The Ultimate Guide *to* great Mentorship

HarperCollins
LEADERSHIP

AN IMPRINT OF HarperCollins

The Ultimate Guide *to great* Mentorship

13 ROLES TO MAKING A TRUE IMPACT

Scott Jeffrey Miller

Published by HarperCollins Leadership, an imprint of HarperCollins Focus LLC.

Any internet addresses, phone numbers, or company or product information printed in this book are offered as a resource and are not intended in any way to be or to imply an endorsement by HarperCollins Leadership, nor does HarperCollins Leadership vouch for the existence, content, or services of these sites, phone numbers, companies, or products beyond the life of this book.

ISBN 978-1-4002-4226-9 (eBook)
ISBN 978-1-4002-4218-4 (TP)

Library of Congress Control Number: 2023931459

Printed in the United States of America
23 24 25 26 27 LBC 6 5 4 3 2

Contents

Contents

Introduction

When HarperCollins Leadership first approached me about authoring a book on mentoring, I was still coalescing the vision for the ten-year, ten-volume series I'm writing titled *Master Mentors: 30 Transformative Insights from Our Greatest Minds*. I'd just finished launching volumes 1 and 2 and had made appearances on more than two hundred podcasts, television shows, and radio programs as part of the book series' launch and ongoing marketing campaign. And the common questions nearly every host and interviewer wanted me to address were often less about the individual mentors I'd featured in the first books and more about the actual process of mentoring: how to select one, how to become one, what to do and not do on both sides, what mentors get right and wrong, and how to recover when conversations don't go as planned. I was frequently asked if mentoring was still relevant in a post-pandemic and increasingly hybrid/virtual work world. When does it go sideways? How do mentors deal with unprepared or overly demanding mentees? The questions seemed endless and interesting and I had an answer for all of them (imagine that . . .).

So I went to work outlining and codifying my point of view on mentoring, recognizing that other books have been written about this topic and by well-qualified authors, including the leadership icon John Maxwell (whom I've interviewed for the *On Leadership with Scott Miller* podcast). As I built my book architecture and drew on my own three decades as a mentor and mentee, I quickly realized I wanted to focus on the many roles mentors play, and specifically on how they differ based on the mentor-mentee dynamic. I identified fifteen roles I thought were important and when I presented them to my early group of advisors who read all my pre-released manuscripts, most of them about passed out. They told me fifteen was a death march, and I absolutely had to narrow the list to a more manageable number. Like eight. Or, at the most, ten. But never fifteen.

I agreed.

I set about clarifying my thoughts on each role and determining which ones were duplicates and could be eliminated or collapsed into others. But a funny thing happened on the way to winnowing the roles—they took on a clearer distinction and seemed worthy of inclusion. With some tightening, I landed on thirteen (admittedly, even that was a little painful). Of course, even then, some roles may seem similar to each other with only nuanced differences. Others will feel distinctly different in their goals and applications. I think your own point of view on the differences and similarities will come to life once you meet with individual mentees and experience their own unique personalities, fears, joys, and perspectives. My intent is to give you a road map for all the roles I think you'll be asked to play, consciously or even unconsciously, as you mentor.

I think maybe later, after reading this book, you might say to yourself: *Oh, now I see some nuances between this role and the other that Scott was talking about.*

At least that's my hope.

So, my advance apologies for intentionally violating the "magical number seven" rule. I think it's more important you build your awareness about all thirteen roles even if your brain can't recall the list as easily as if there were fewer. That's why we have books. Maybe I'm insolent or maybe I'm onto something valuable for each of you. I'm sure you'll let me know in your Amazon reviews. I read them all . . . after a few glasses of champagne. Surprisingly, I don't care as much after the cork pops.

Here are some quick tips on how to make the most of this book:

First, the book was written nearly exclusively for the mentor, not the mentee. I don't think there are any secrets mentees can't know about, but I'd caution you about how you choose to share what you're reading, as you want your adoption of the roles to be natural and aligned with your style and never feel contrived, awkward, or obvious that you're moving from one to another.

Second, the thirteen roles are not all going to happen in every mentoring relationship. And they certainly don't happen all at the same time or in any specific sequence per se (with a couple of minor exceptions). My intent is to equip you with the knowledge, awareness, preparedness, and enhanced skills (and even scripts) so as topics and circumstances arise, you can identify a role that's relevant and worth adopting at any moment.

Third, I focus on each role in two sections: Chapters (for reading and absorbing) and Captures (for reflection and note-taking). My recommendation is to read the chapter and highlight anything you think will be valuable for where you are in your own mentoring journey—including insights, phrases, questions, or statements you might like to integrate into your conversations.

Each chapter aligns to a role and is organized into similar parts:

- A description of the role
- The goal
- Upsides
- Downsides
- Skills
- A narrative aligned to the identified skills
- Video illustration (that's the QR code) of me, the author, highlighting key insights and sharing bonus material in a short video

Then after you've read the role-specific Chapter, use the Captures section for taking notes before, during, and after your mentoring sessions or as a pull-through of any insights you'd like to remember to draw upon later.

Finally, visit greatmentorship.com for more tools and resources to help perfect your mentoring contribution.

Here are some potential watch-outs to consider as you're reading about each of the roles:

- I use a lot—I mean a lot—of metaphors. I hope you like them and find them valuable. If you don't (and some of you won't), keep reading and leave them behind. I certainly don't want you getting hijacked by what you think is a distracting metaphor. It's how I speak and thus how I write. At least you know you're getting an authentic Scott Jeffrey Miller experience.

- You'll likely find some of the roles very similar to each other and may even struggle to see substantive differences. In some cases they are subtle and the differences might come to you later, even after reading and hopefully in the midst of your mentoring sessions. Don't get hung up on similarities—keep reading to the next chapter or role if you are spending too much time trying to differentiate.

- At the end of the book, what I hope you take away is awareness of when you choose to function in a particular role. Make them your own. Maybe you decide to choose three or four roles and stick with them for much, most, or all of your mentoring time. That's your call. Don't get bogged down in a quandary of "am I in *this* role or *that* role?" Just the awareness that there are roles and some of them will come more naturally to you and be more valuable to your mentee is mission accomplished. There is an optional card deck and accompanying journal available at greatmentorship.com that have been designed as tools to help bring these roles to life in an organized and thoughtful way across your unique mentorship journey.

Your potential for positively influencing your mentee is incalculable. In fact, you will never know the full extent of your impact, because your mentee doesn't always fully appreciate or even understand it themselves. That's OK. Just trust that your investment is likely changing a life. Maybe even your own.

The Ultimate Guide *to* *great* Mentorship

Role 1:
The Revealer

The Revealer works like a paleontologist, delicately brushing away the metaphorical dust and debris to reveal their mentee's passions, talents, fears, and goals. The Revealer delicately uncovers what's just beneath the surface and/or digs deeper as appropriate. In essence, they work to uncover so others can discover—all while remaining hyperaware of their own footprints (personalities) in the sand.

The Goal

To lead the mentee's awareness, progress, and growth through precise exploration and discovery. And along the way ensure their own style and approach doesn't overwhelm or distract.

The Upside When The Revealer Role Is Employed Well

- Surfaces important facts and feelings that can help or hinder personal effectiveness and engagement
- Provides a framework for a mentor to lean into their own stylistic strengths or work through and around weaknesses
- Helps a mentee feel safe and appropriately vulnerable so they can become "comfortable with being uncomfortable"

The Downside When The Revealer Role Is Abdicated

A mentee can easily shut down, feel overwhelmed, or become intimidated by a heavy-handed mentoring approach. As a result, they can often pull back, obfuscate, or even abandon the relationship altogether.

Key Revealer Skills

- Know the "dig site"—what the mentee is trying to accomplish and the environment in which they are trying to accomplish it
- Employ patience and deliberate thinking
- Remain hyperaware of your own footprints (your default personality style)
- Explore with an inquisitive and gentle approach

Know the Dig Site—What the Mentee Is Trying to Accomplish and the Environment in Which They Are Trying to Accomplish It

In many facets as a mentor, you're leading an excavation. Uncovering. Revealing. Retrieving. Metaphorically, you're bringing to life what may be buried beneath the surface as it relates to the passions and goals of your mentee. Enter the paleontologist-like Revealer. The Revealer doesn't helicopter into a site and whip up a cloud of dust and debris. They understand that a mentee's goals, like a dig site, can be easily trodden over, disrupted, or even demolished. The Revealer carefully enters this space with their tools, expertise, and an inquisitive nature in tow. They're discreet and delicate about both *where* they're stepping and *why*.

They certainly don't use jackhammers and backhoes! At least not early on.

The Revealer understands that a mentee is often part of an existing team complete with norms, cultural expectations, and unique faux pas from each member. The Revealer, as paleontologist, isn't interested in blowing up or changing the site in which they work— they are a precise excavator focused on going deep with their mentee.

The Revealer is always aware that the environment matters. For example, if you're mentoring someone in your organization whose "dig site" is contemplating an upward career trajectory, they may or may not know if they're even in the right culture for them to succeed. If they're more entrepreneurial-minded, they may be confused as to whether they should secure a small business loan for future seed funds or, more boldly, approach a venture capitalist or angel investor.

Everyone's dig site is going to be different. It's important when you're in the role of The Revealer that you're hyperaware of your own prejudices, expectations, preconceived eventualities, and so on. As a mentor, your collective life experiences often provide valuable shortcuts for you to make snap decisions about how to move forward—and that is a dangerous competency you'll be tempted to employ. Proceed with enormous caution, and do not assume you know what you're uncovering. Even paleontologists sometimes don't know whether the first bone is going to be from a brontosaurus, a pterodactyl, or an undiscovered species. Repeat: You don't announce, "Eureka, we've found a T. rex!" with mere millimeters of the fossil exposed. You shouldn't presuppose anything. Later in the process, maybe, but not in the beginning. Revealers always learn the lay of the land first.

Employ Patience and Deliberate Thinking

Revealers are patient and deliberate people—or summon these characteristics if they don't come naturally. They don't always know what they're going to uncover and so they remain open to what might reveal itself. They may have an inkling, but they're careful not to let assumptions dictate their process or discoveries. They seek understanding and discovery through delicate brushstrokes and not hammer blows.

Depending on the mentee's personality, socioeconomic background, education, goals, confidence, fears, and so on, you may need to brush longer and more delicately than you otherwise would in your own career or life. Or with your spouse or partner. Or children. (Or perhaps the recalibration you learn to employ as a mentor in professional settings might bleed over into your personal life and also improve those relationships and your influence as well. Just sayin' . . .)

As The Revealer, it's vital to meet the mentee where they are in terms of professional sophistication, maturity, life experience, and even intellectual processing speed. What may seem like an obvious choice to you may emotionally paralyze them and necessitate a higher level of patience on your part while they work through their own contemplative process. You're there to help uncover the best direction for *them* based on *their* journey.

Let me repeat that. The best direction for *them*.

Not for *you*.

And not how you imagine it should be if *you* were them. In fact, that's a great watch-out. Resist saying, "Well, if I were you . . ."

You cannot be them.

Ever.

You may, however, state, "When I was faced with a similar decision, here's how I approached it . . . But again, I am not you and you are not me so . . ."

I repeat: You may not pretend you are your mentee by saying, "If I were you . . ."

Remain Hyperaware of Your Own Footprints (Your Default Personality Style)

Revealers are ever mindful of their own footprints. They don't charge in headstrong by purposely setting the tone or determining the outcomes—which can be tempting when most mentors are seasoned leaders often used to and comfortable with determining the goals, measures, and strategies for their team and colleagues. Instead, Revealers intentionally meet the mentee where they are, as they intuitively know it's their job to "Seek First to Understand . . ." the first half of Habit 5 from Dr. Stephen R. Covey's seminal book, *The 7 Habits of Highly Effective People.* This is critical, as many mentees, especially the more junior (by age or stature), can't always articulate their passions and goals at the outset of a mentoring relationship. It's entirely possible that your mentee may enter their first session with no specific end in mind or change it midway through your sessions based on your mentoring process.

Resist the very natural temptation to rush in and tell. Keep your brush in hand and save the pickax for another day. You'll likely find an opportunity for it later, just not now.

Explore with an Inquisitive and Gentle Approach

The Revealer role is first for a reason. At this early phase, they're using their metaphorical brush and excavation tools to sweep away the surface dust to get a sense of whom and what they're dealing with.

Your primary job as The Revealer is to help uncover the *mentee's* feelings, perceptions, strengths, fears, and misconceptions about their own potential by consistently being mindful of the fact that you're not them. Perhaps I'm belaboring this point, however, of all the counsel I will offer you in this book, this has the greatest potential for making a true impact with your mentee: Be mindful of your footprint, as it's larger than you think it is. It's drawn from your own life and career journey and manifests in a variety of ways, including your vocabulary, confidence, intellect, humor, mathematical skills, charm, deductive reasoning skills, intellectual processing speed, and so on. We all have a set of experiences and talents that enabled us to thrive and survive the politics and cultural nuances of our own employers and varied careers. These experiences and talents may have become second nature to you, but without stopping and carefully determining if they're also existent in your mentee, they may diminish and intimidate your mentee more than validate them. Additionally, the paleontologist never turns the brush on themselves—they never want their own fears, doubts, or unfulfilled dreams clouding the mentee's journey. Similar in nature to how some parents live vicariously through their children, mentors should never make the same mistake with their mentees.

Help your mentee discover and name their strengths and weaknesses. Identify areas of growth that may be a repeated stumbling block (or a one-time hurdle) and resist the temptation to develop or focus on specific skills that may not lead them to accomplishing their goal(s). Said another way, a mentor's ultimate role is to help identify what a mentee is trying to accomplish and build. And often that involves the delicate discovery work to identify what they're avoiding, neglecting, ignoring, or wrongly fixated on as well.

The Revealer is an expert at creating a safe environment, allowing their mentee to feel comfortable sharing their uncertainty, fears, and even lack of vision or strategy. They may not know what they want out of life or a career—or even the mentoring relationship itself. Your role is to make them feel comfortable being uncomfortable.

The Revealer Role and Me

Simply and crudely put, I get shit done. Most people know to either get on board with Scott or get out of his way, because I'm known as a force of nature and I'm not typically stopping for anyone. It's my brand and works in everyone's favor about 85 percent of the time. (As for the other 15 percent? Keep reading.)

I have naturally high (meteoric) energy. I'm sometimes described as indefatigable. Truth is, I didn't fully come to realize this as a liability until late into my forties, when my wife, Stephanie, in one of her continual interventions with me, practiced some "straight talk" and told me how fatiguing it can be. My energy. My voice level. My sense of omniscience and if you just do it my way, exactly as I prescribe, all will work out (exactly as *I* envision it). She reminded me that I talk on the speakerphone in the car the same way I do to an arena of seven thousand people—when she's sitting in the passenger seat, two feet from me. And that she finds it especially annoying. Exhausting. And likes me less as a result. (Marriage ain't easy.)

This propensity to annoy people with my energy and voice level was further proven to me when I was once in Alabama leading a work session for clients. I was greeting participants as they arrived for the 8:00 a.m. start, and I was ready to rock and roll. You see, if you know anything about me or follow me on social media, you know I wake up at 4:00 a.m. every day. Seven days a week, I am a very earlier riser, as mornings are my peak time to think, work, and deploy my creativity. (Now, before you feel lessened by this discipline of mine, know that I am also horizontal and sound asleep every night by 9:30 p.m. and have never, ever, seen the results of a thirty-minute episode of *House Hunters International*. I always fall asleep before they announce their selection—it's so frustrating.)

Back to the story from Alabama. I distinctly remember bounding up to a woman who'd just sat down with her coffee before the opening and introducing myself. "GOOD MORNING. GREAT TO MEET YOU. MY NAME IS SCOTT AND I WILL BE YOUR FACILITATOR TODAY. WHAT'S YOUR NAME?"

Now brace yourself for her response. She looks up at me, makes deliberate, piercing eye contact, and says, like a police officer writing a ticket at the end of a long shift: "It's way too early for this. You are too close and in my space, and you need to back yourself up."

Gulp.

Nothing about her word choice, tone, or body language inferred she was kidding either. I thought, *There's a thousand ways you could have said that more delicately, lady . . .* but rather than vocalizing it, I just smiled, acknowledged her response, and moved on to my next high-energy encounter (victim). *It was her issue, not mine . . .*

Or so I deluded myself into thinking. And thinking I did, reflecting on it much of that day and the flight home. And that night. And the next morning.

Up until that point in my career, no one had ever had the courage to call me out. Or if they had, I'd missed it (more likely ignored it). I completely lacked perspective about how forceful I was, or less delicately put, how annoying my energy, confidence, presence, or volume could be, even when well-intended.

From that pivotal morning in Alabama and with the additional (constant) counsel from Stephanie and others, I've become much more self-aware about my "entrance" tone, as well as other encounters where I need to be more mindful of calibrating my voice, tone, pitch, energy, and even how much confidence I project for each environment I'm in and each person I'm talking to.

Now this might seem like Interpersonal Communications 101, but we all can benefit from a revisit with our own styles. I know people who have such little self-awareness about their personality style that it's embarrassing—for them. Perhaps it's their need to always be right. Or they don't know when to let others shine or stand out. Could be their incessant interrupting. Or dominance that serves them professionally as a strength but in relationships with others is diminishing and crushing even. We don't always realize our impact on people—positive and negative. Our well-crafted questions can turn into an interrogation. Or our discomfort with silence can manifest as a pummeling of questions and comments to "keep the conversation moving."

Whatever your default style, if your main reference point is yourself, your mentee can become unintentionally minimized and intimidated. They begin to form quick impressions and defensive responses. Too often in mentor-mentee relationships, it's the mentee trying to match the mentor's personality, speed, and style. And that's likely going to be the default culture of your relationship in the beginning (welcome to the dynamic and hierarchy of professional relationships). However, you never want your mentee thinking any of these thoughts:

- I'm going to have to choose my words more carefully.
- I'm going to have to really ramp up today to match their energy.
- I must hold my own intellectually on this topic or they'll think I'm incompetent.

The Revealer understands they're inherently in a position of dominance and carefully works to diminish the effect. As a Revealer, the more you understand the unintended consequences of this hierarchical dynamic, the more you may need to modify your style as you brush away the sand and debris from an important "artifact." Here you must learn the power of your presence, personality, tools, experience, vocabulary, and life knowledge and then carefully calibrate and apply such to each mentoring situation.

Of course, you can overcorrect too far and become someone you're not. I've done this myself: sensing a mentee's apprehension and then, as the metaphorical paleontologist, offering a toothbrush and a hand fan and announcing, "See you in four months. Hope you discover a dinosaur . . . or whatever it might happen to be." My thinking was that if I intentionally backed away, they would figure it all out without me. Be mindful not to swing the pendulum too far one way or another, but rather balance your natural style with what also builds trust and rapport with your mentee based on their style. The key is knowing your audience (mentee). Get to know their personality a bit before yours comes fully out. Now, don't misunderstand me, it's imperative that your mentee connect with you and find some similarities and commonalities with who you both are. Just be thoughtful that you become relatable and likable, not "imitate-*able*."

Another frequent challenge may present itself, and that's having vastly different personalities, communication styles, and thinking processes. One of my most recent mentees is a prime example. We don't work together professionally, in the same organization or in any capacity. She works for a client organization and reached out to me individually. We're different in every aspect. Gender. Age. Race.

Education. (She has a PhD, and I . . . well . . . don't). Her children are in college, and mine are in elementary school. She works in the medical industry, and I once went to the hospital for a shot. Our fields of experience are as vastly different as are our personalities and communication styles. She is measured. Thoughtful. Contemplative . . . you get the point.

For this mentor-mentee relationship to be effective—for both of us—I've come to ask myself, "Is the question I'm going to ask helping her or helping me? What's my motive? How do I want to show up? What does she need from me? Because what she needs from me might be different from what someone else needs from me. Because our styles are so diametrically opposed, I have to discipline myself to both appreciate her style and intentionally move toward it. Not a natural experience for me when for over three decades I served as a senior leader of people where the majority of them moved closer to my style (welcome to life as a leader in the 1990s and early 2000s while striving to adapt to being a leader in 2023 and beyond).

In the role of Revealer, I've deliberately tried to match her energy level by lowering the volume of my voice in our calls. I've become a little more patient as I try to keep an inquisitive mindset and reject the idea I need a prescribed end in mind during each of our sessions. In this case, it's me who's had to become comfortable being uncomfortable, not always knowing where we're going. This, ideally, will become clearer as the relationship matures.

Where I might typically force a choice or decision in a professional leadership setting, I now invite her to ponder an opportunity for the week ahead and come back seven days later with a decision. (I may well die within the week, so this is completely counterintuitive for me.) Remember, I'm the guy who gets shit done.

Please don't think I'm diminishing this extremely competent and accomplished person. In many settings, she would smoke me intellectually, and her candor and insights always stay with me after our mentoring calls. I always leave inspired by her grace and elegance and often attempt to enter a new day modeling much of her measured approach (at least for a few minutes . . .). But that's the beauty of The Revealer—like a paleontologist, they're not always sure what exact artifact is hidden in the dust. But they carefully, methodically, and patiently move bits of dirt here and there until they find what's hidden. Sometimes it's what they intend and sometimes it's a surprise. But that surprise can often have reciprocal benefits to both mentor and mentee. Thus, The Revealer is always on the lookout to learn something new.

I was recently in Rome at the Vatican and St. Peter's Basilica with my family, and during our tour, we came across the famous *Pietà* sculpture carved by Michelangelo in the fifteenth century. It's a masterpiece and the only sculpture he signed. It's truly breathtaking.

Here's the thing though: The dude created it out of a block of marble—in just over a year.

You are *not* going to create a *Pietà* of your mentee in eight, ten, or twelve sessions. The Revealer implicitly understands this. So take a breath . . . and then another. Your work in this role is designed to build rapport, safety, and trust. And don't worry, you'll get your chance to ask piercing questions, get to the root cause, and peel the onion as The Questioner (role #4). But this isn't likely the opening role you'll need to play. More often than not, it will be that of The Revealer. So be patient for now (and believe me, I know how hard and unintuitive this can feel).

Put away the pickaxe and jackhammer and gently dust with your brush. Then look back and be careful that you haven't mistaken your footprints for theirs.

Captures—Additional Tools

PRE-MENTORING REFLECTION

Consider those who have played The Revealer role in your life (this might include formal mentors, colleagues, parents, friends, teachers, and ecclesiastical leaders). Review which of the Key Revealer Skills illustrated in the chapter opening that they demonstrated and describe the impact in your life:

_____

_____

_____

_____

_____

Role 1: The Revealer

Capture the "big ideas" you have about The Revealer role. Consider your own mentoring experiences. What in life has prepared you for this role? What might you need to do to prepare more? What can you adopt from the previous exercise? Write your thoughts below:

_____

_____

_____

_____

_____

IN-THE-MOMENT MENTORING PROMPTS

Revisit the questions and key insights found throughout The Revealer chapter. These could include both questions for the mentee or reflection questions to help you with your mentoring mindset. Choose which feel the most relevant to an upcoming mentoring session and write them below. If the questions are reflective in nature, take a moment to answer them for yourself.

Mentee Questions

Question 1:

_____

Question 2:

_____

Question 3:

_____

Question 4:

_____

Mentor Reflection Questions

Question 1:

_____

Answer:

_____

Question 2:

_____

Answer:

_____

Question 3:

_____

Answer:

_____

Question 4:

_____

Answer:

_____

POST-MENTORING LEARNING

Following your mentoring session, think back to how things went when adopting The Revealer role. Some roles may feel more natural to you than others, but they all benefit from objectively assessing what worked, what didn't, and what you can learn as a result.

1. **Circle the answer that best corresponds to this statement:**
   "The Revealer role was effective for me as a mentor during the mentoring session."

   a. Strongly agree

   b. Agree

   c. Neutral

   d. Disagree

   e. Strongly disagree

2. **Circle the answer that best corresponds to this statement:**
   "In the mentoring session, I achieved The Revealer goal: 'To lead the mentee's awareness, progress, and growth through precise exploration and discovery. And along the way ensure their own style and approach doesn't overwhelm or distract.'"

   a. Strongly agree

   b. Agree

   c. Neutral

   d. Disagree

   e. Strongly disagree

3. **Explore the "why" behind your answers.** Consider what worked and didn't in your mentoring session. What should you stop or start doing? What might you do less or more of? If you found gaps in your ability to execute this role, what can you do to close them? Capture your learning from this session and anything that, on reflection, could help you grow to be more comfortable and capable in this role:

    _____

    _____

    _____

    _____

    _____

Role 2: The Boundary Setter

The Boundary Setter creates the parameters of the mentoring relationship. They do this up front and as early as possible so that the proper guardrails exist and the mentoring journey can be efficient, effective, and safe.

The Goal

To set clear boundaries about expectations, what the mentoring relationship is and isn't, and the roles the mentor and mentee will play and won't.

The Upside When The Boundary Setter Role Is Employed Well

- Both parties understand the scope of the mentoring relationship
- Saves time having to deal with issues in the moment that could have been mitigated through setting expectations early on
- Helps the mentee understand their role and expectations for the mentoring sessions themselves
- Provides an early warning for mismatched expectations between a mentor and mentee
- Offers a novice (and even experienced) mentee a clear picture of what lines can be blurred, and which shouldn't be crossed

The Downside When The Boundary Setter Role Is Abdicated

Mentoring sessions are more likely to wander off topic, be at risk for unintentional and improper requests, and become unproductive (or worse).

Key Boundary Setter Skills

- Designate duration and frequency
- Confirm the agenda
- Establish roles and responsibilities
- Set boundaries

- Call a time-out when needed
- Make and keep commitments
- Address violations
- Pull the plug if necessary

The Boundary Setter is a role that is unique in that it is typically set up at the beginning of the mentor-mentee relationship, perhaps in some cases even before you enter the role of The Revealer. Then, it may need to be revisited (reinforced) if a mentee skirts the established boundaries. Setting such parameters for the mentoring relationship is essential. Sometimes, if you're part of an organizational initiative, that may be done for you. But you will still want to reiterate them and protect both you and your mentee from any embarrassing or overreaching conversations. To quote the famed author and leadership expert Blaine Lee, "Nearly all, if not all, conflict in life, comes from mismatched or unfulfilled expectations."

Designate Duration and Frequency

How long and often you meet with your mentee will vary on the structure of your organization and if they have a formal mentoring program in place. Maybe they've invited (conscripted) you to be a mentor and have outlined a session structure, including how long your engagement may last. If that's not your circumstance, give some thought to how long you want to commit yourself. For example, you might set the expectation that you're willing to join for six to eight sessions, and if there's a compelling reason to continue, you can announce that as the initial batch is ending. My best counsel is to target forty-five minutes for each session, but hold a full hour on your calendar. It's difficult to surface weighty issues and address them in under forty-five minutes, and there are always detours (and sometimes those detours are enormously valuable to the relationship). Your mentoring sessions are likely best done in person or on video, and I strongly advise against audio-only calls unless the established rapport and nature of the conversation lends itself to that environment.

Confirm the Agenda

I believe this responsibility lies solely with the mentee and not the mentor. If your mentee lacks the maturity, experience, or skills to lead this, teach them how to create a cogent agenda, but don't take it over for them. As the mentor, ensure the first discussion sets the standard that the mentee will need to join future sessions (in person or virtually) with a well-thought-out agenda based on what can be accomplished in the agreed-upon time. The mentee will need to pace themselves and leave time for the mentor's advice, potentially having to learn from a previous session what's realistic in terms of topics covered. It's helpful to model what setting a valuable agenda looks like and how to "park" items that can't be resolved and carry them forward to the next meeting—or intentionally abandon them. You will know quickly how to balance your counsel based on their sophistication.

Establish Roles and Responsibilities

Depending on your mentee and the situation, it may be useful to clarify the specific role you intend to take. Consider sharing the temptations you'll work to resist, including confusing your passions, fears, and skills with theirs. Let the mentee know there may be times when you're quieter or more reflective than they know you to be or wish you were during these meetings. I don't think it's necessary or valuable to apprise them that there are thirteen roles you might play (or not play) and outline what they all are. However, it could be organically helpful to say something like, "One of the many roles a mentor plays is what's called The Challenger. In this role, a mentor decides when to push back on a concept or path that they think might not be best for their mentee. I feel like this is an opportunity for me to be The Challenger, so let's talk for a few minutes about . . ."

Set Boundaries

This is likely the most important part of this chapter and maybe even the entire book. What's the *second-quickest* way for a mentee to irritate their mentor? Commit to doing something and then showing up the next week empty-handed. This is a complete waste of the mentor's time (that's you) and I think you should clearly address it up front.

What is the *quickest* way to irritate a mentor? Ask them to play a role beyond mentor. I implore you to set this boundary up front. Clarify what you, as their mentor, *will* and *won't* offer. Roles a mentor generally does *not* take on include:

- Marriage/relationship counselor
- Physician/nutritionist
- Substance abuse counselor
- Lawyer, CPA, or investment advisor
- Grief counselor
- Champion
- Ally
- Supporter
- Benefactor
- Professional reference
- Loan officer/banker

Under rare circumstances should a mentee ask their mentor to make a connection to someone in their network. Or fund a project. That's what LinkedIn and banks are for, not mentors. If you're being asked for advice in an area that requires specialized training or certifications, simply advise your mentee to seek answers from such professionals.

Finally, you should take a position whether you intend (or are even interested) in making your professional network available to your mentee. Set and communicate this boundary as well (see The Connector, role #12, for more).

Setting boundaries early helps save you from getting into a situation where you have to say no. Now, having said all that, if you take a liking to your mentee and you choose to reassess your position on any of the roles outlined above, that's completely your call. But proceed with caution and consider how and when you will communicate that the boundaries have changed. Remember what our wise parents said, "Good fences make good neighbors."

Call a Time-out When Needed

No, you don't get to send your mentee to their room, but sometimes you may need to stop the conversation, even abruptly, if the train is going off the tracks. I've addressed this in other roles (particularly The Flagger, role #9), but there will be occasions when a well-timed interruption is necessary for you to bring clarity and even sanity to an important topic. Keep in mind you are not the SEC, FBI, CIA, IRS, NSA, or any other three-letter agency. However, your role as The Boundary Setter may necessitate you "going on record" to dispute or refute something you know to be factually wrong or if they shared an idea that is ethically or morally suspect. Don't hesitate to step into The Flagger role to interject that you'd like to stop for a moment and take a deeper dive into a specific topic they are discussing. Your decision to gain clarity provides the mentee with the knowledge that you disagree, and provides you, as the mentor, with some air cover if, in an organizationally led mentoring initiative, you're asked about your previous discussions and you need a defense. The chance is .001 percent that you'll ever encounter that type of issue, but not zero (and as we know, sometimes crazy shows up when we least expect it, and it's best to have a game plan ready).

Make and Keep Commitments

This applies to both of you, but likely most to your mentee.

First, there may be rare occasions for you, as the mentor, to make commitments in between sessions, calls, or meetings. Perhaps you quote an article you'll forward, offer to share a research finding, suggest a sample résumé, or source a slide deck or business plan for review. Whatever it is you commit to doing, be thoughtful about the slippery slope of overpromising and underdelivering. In most mentoring relationships, your time, wisdom, and experience are 100 percent of what you bring to your mentee. Your mentee, however, will make many commitments and must be held completely accountable for all of them. This doesn't mean you become the Commitment Cop, but it's important for their brand and your perception of them that you remind them that how they make and keep commitments during your mentoring relationship shows you their level of seriousness and ultimately becomes their reputation—in life. Again, this is best clarified up front. Perhaps even remind your mentee that everyone has a brand—a collection of all the decisions they make and commitments they keep . . . and don't.

Address Violations

Violations typically present themselves as missed calls and meetings, chronic tardiness, consistently being unprepared and not delivering on commitments made in previous meetings. You will need to decide how you will address this in the moment, but like all the boundaries you set as the mentor, this is better addressed and thus minimized by discussing it up front. Don't underestimate the power of clarifying your expectations on the first call. This might haunt them a bit and that's just fine.

Pull the Plug If Necessary

In extreme circumstances, the mentoring fit may just not be right. I'd be willing to bet this will become clear in the first engagement, and if not then, absolutely by the second. You will need to determine the best way to pull the plug. Not on *them*, as a mentee, but on *you* as their mentor. Forcing an extreme misfit can do more harm than good, and you must decide how and when to exit the situation. Just like when you know a new hire is wrong for the role and you've made a mistake hiring them, you often need to terminate them quickly. I think the same applies here. Cut your (and their) losses if you're convinced it's the wrong fit. Certainly, you could choose to stick it out and either suffer through or see if it improves, but as in life, unaddressed issues rarely improve and never resolve themselves.

The Boundary Setter Role and Me

A common discussion (and when I say "discussion" of course I mean "argument") I have with my wife, Stephanie, is when we're driving in the car together, typically on a highway, and she's telling me to slow down. For a decade-plus, my response has been, "I'm just going with the flow of traffic." This seemed to be a reasonable defense until a Utah traffic safety commercial started airing locally, mocking the phrase, "I'm just going with the flow." Which simply means I need a new phrase—not a reconsideration of my speed, of course!

Relate?

In life, there's what's known as "the letter of the law" and "the spirit of the law" compliance. Some laws, fortunately, the majority of us would never even consider breaking. Other people might consider them as "strong suggestions." Kind of like how my friend and colleague Ty Schmidt jokingly refers to annoyingly placed stop signs in the middle of nowhere as "Stoptional." I'll let you determine which are which for you, but I think it's valuable as we end our focus on this role to talk about which boundaries you've set up front might work their way toward "spirit" versus "letter" of the law flexibility as your mentee demonstrates increased respect and maturity.

For much of my life, I've had a strong stutter. With speech therapy and lots of hard work, I've nearly conquered it. One of my speech coaches works with me not only on my stutter but my speaking and presentation skills, which include components like body language, hand gestures, my physical movement, eye contact, and perfecting my storytelling skills. I spend a full day with her every year, and we rent a massive auditorium (like three thousand–plus seats) and she beats me up. I deliver the same keynote from the stage to three thousand empty seats (except her sitting in the middle with a blow horn) and she tears me down and builds me back up—multiple times throughout the sessions, hopefully making me better than when I arrived that morning. Her favorite words are "NO" and "STOP." I love her, truly.

She teaches (pounds) the principles of great delivery into me with each session and then after she's certain I'm scared shitless about deviating from her standards, she reminds me of the following. "Once you fully understand and master the rules, only then can you choose to break them." For example, when you're presenting on stage or in front of any size audience, it's forbidden (a word she would use) to put your hands in your pockets. It tends to draw the audience's eyes toward your groin (not generally a positive). Which is also why one of her rules is that nothing can be in your pocket when you're presenting for fear you might choose to fiddle with it and . . . you can probably figure out why that's not a great look.

Her point is less about NEVER put your hands in your pockets, but more about being aware of the consequences. If you have, in fact, removed everything from your pockets and need a short resting place for one of your hands (because perhaps you're holding in the other a microphone, marker, slide advancer, or paper), then with full acknowledgment that you're going to put your hand in your pocket for one or maybe two minutes at the most, you may do so. But it can't be a repeated habit, or a constant default location for your hand. And you must then remove it.

Her overall point is well taken. The Boundary Setter is about establishing rules. But after some work together, earned maturity, and increasing level of trust, you can help your mentee know when the "hard and fast" line you *never* cross is actually a bit "fuzzy" and they can carefully and intentionally own the consequences for stepping over it, or even being invited by you to do so.

Captures—Additional Tools

PRE-MENTORING REFLECTION

Consider those who have played The Boundary Setter role in your life (this might include formal mentors, colleagues, parents, friends, teachers, and ecclesiastical leaders). Review which of the Key Boundary Setter Skills illustrated in the chapter opening that they demonstrated and describe the impact in your life:

_____

_____

_____

_____

Capture the "big ideas" you have about The Boundary Setter role. Consider your own mentoring experiences. What in life has prepared you for this role? What might you need to do to prepare more? What can you adopt from the previous exercise? Write your thoughts below:

_____

_____

_____

_____

_____

IN-THE-MOMENT MENTORING PROMPTS

Revisit the questions and key insights found throughout The Boundary Setter chapter. These could include both questions for the mentee or reflection questions to help you with your mentoring mindset. Choose which feel the most relevant to an upcoming mentoring session and write them below. If the questions are reflective in nature, take a moment to answer them for yourself.

Mentee Questions

Question 1:

_____

Question 2:

_____

Question 3:

_____

Question 4:

_____

Mentor Reflection Questions

Question 1:

_____

Answer:

_____

Question 2:

_____

Answer:

_____

Question 3:

_____

Answer:

_____

Question 4:

_____

Answer:

_____

POST-MENTORING LEARNING

Following your mentoring session, think back to how things went when adopting The Boundary Setter role. Some roles may feel more natural to you than others, but they all benefit from objectively assessing what worked, what didn't, and what you can learn as a result.

1. *Circle the answer that best corresponds to this statement:* "The Boundary Setter role was effective for me as a mentor during the mentoring session."

   a. Strongly agree

   b. Agree

   c. Neutral

   d. Disagree

   e. Strongly disagree

2. *Circle the answer that best corresponds to this statement:* "In the mentoring session, I achieved the Boundary Setter goal: 'To set clear boundaries about expectations, what the mentoring relationship is and isn't, and the roles the mentor and mentee will play and won't.'"

   a. Strongly agree

   b. Agree

   c. Neutral

   d. Disagree

   e. Strongly disagree

3. **Explore the "why" behind your answers.** Consider what worked and didn't in your mentoring session. What should you stop or start doing? What might you do less or more of? If you found gaps in your ability to execute this role, what can you do to close them? Capture your learning from this session and anything that, on reflection, could help you grow to be more comfortable and capable in this role:

_____

_____

_____

_____

_____

Role 3:
The Absorber

Second in priority to The Revealer is The Absorber. The Absorber recognizes that the best mentors are active listeners. They foster an environment of psychological safety where mentees feel heard, understood, and valued.

The Goal

To invest your focused time and attention into your mentee through active listening, empathy, and intentional focus.

The Upside When The Absorber Role Is Employed Well

- Creates a high-trust environment where mentees feel safe to be vulnerable, heard, and understood

- Builds an expectation and experience that the mentee can share "unfiltered" what's on their mind and work through it without judgment
- Helps mentees discover their unique and valuable genius

The Downside When The Absorber Role Is Abdicated

Mentors confuse declaration with dialogue, trading short-term efficiencies for the long-term benefits that come from investing in and hearing what their mentees have to say.

Key Absorber Skills

- Get out of selling mode
- Avoid the "If I were you . . ." trap
- Learn your mentee's genius (and resist shaping it into yours)
- Listen and absorb as an active listener
- Practice intentional focus and empathic listening
- Stop interrupting
- Be gentle on yourself and know when to be prescriptive

In my thirty-plus professional years in the leadership industry, I see a strong correlation between powerful leaders and their lack of listening skills.

Yep, you read that right.

Keep in mind, *powerful* doesn't mean successful, effective, or respected. Sure, such leaders bring intensity when dictating strategy, driving momentum, or pushing toward a goal. They can be forces of nature who do whatever it takes to achieve results—regardless of the cultural consequences. Perhaps not all bad (if it's 1990) but certainly not all good post-2020. Not that organizations don't benefit from leader-driven strategies, flywheel speed execution, and charismatic personalities, with inexhaustible energy to win in today's highly competitive and challenging marketplaces. These are valuable skills when tempered and used judicially.

Enter The Absorber.

This role requires a probably unnatural level of patience, curiosity, and suspended judgment from mentors. I understand this is not an epiphany for any reader—you need to listen better to be a mentor. Earth-shattering, I know. But to quote my old pal Voltaire, "Common knowledge isn't common practice." Or from my leader and mentor for many years, Dr. Stephen R. Covey, "To know, but not to do, is not to know."

Like many virtuous habits, both the mentor *and* their mentee benefit when a leader can shut up and listen. And if you think you're already good at that, here's a newsflash: You can do better. From delivering hundreds of keynotes and facilitating too-many-to-count consulting and coaching sessions in more than fifty countries, I've come to recognize that listening is likely the most underrated and, plainly put, most difficult leadership skill of them all.

Get Out of Selling Mode

This can feel counterintuitive, as most of the leaders I know are often, if not always, in selling mode. They employ persuasion tactics or have a default style of communication aimed at swaying others to think or do something in a prescribed way. Typically their way.

Selling.

Persuading.

Influencing.

But for leaders who cannot adapt to The Absorber role, it's likely because they're stuck in that selling competency, which is great when driving revenue or needing to push forward a strategy, but a misplaced skill in mentoring. As a mentor, you shouldn't be selling anything, until perhaps much further into your relationship where something is so clear to you that you adopt The Distiller role, #10.

Now is not the time to sell, but to listen and absorb.

Avoid the "If I Were You . . ." Trap

Why is listening so vital to making a true impact as a mentor? Because one of the most dangerous traps you'll find yourself in is speaking the phrase, likely unconsciously, "Well, if I were you . . ." I'm carrying this concept forward from The Revealer because what often gets in the way of listening is drawing upon your own experiences and, in a well-intentioned fashion, wanting to accelerate their learning via your prescription.

It's understandable, but dangerous.

Don't do it.

Not yet.

You are not them and will never be them, so eliminate this thinking and response from your vernacular.

When a mentor says, "If I were you . . ." what they really mean is "You should do this . . . just like me." Mentors hold different mindsets and skill sets and have access to different tools and resources than their mentees, so it's even more of a useless statement. Now, I intend to keep pounding away at this temptation through the entire book, less because of your inclination to say it (although you will be inclined to do so frequently), but because it flows from your mindset, paradigm, and deeply inculcated beliefs of what you would do in any situation. I believe it's quite natural to think and speak through the lens of what we would do. That's our default belief process and how we've gotten stuff done in our lives. The essence of your own success is likely deeply rooted in your personal decision-making tree. Climb that branch? Nope, it broke and sent me tumbling last time. Climb on this branch? Sure, it held me just fine.

So it should hold everyone else fine too—right?!

It's important to remind ourselves how easily we can slip into our comfortable narrative about what we did, what we would do, or how we would approach a situation faced by a mentee. Of course, you'll draw on your experiences in life as a mentor, but this cannot be your default style. Become mindful of how often this happens in your mentoring sessions (or life) and remember your mentee has a very different set of competencies, life experiences, and realms of knowledge than you do. How you would go about pursuing some path in your life may in fact be genius, but it's based on *your* genius and not theirs. And you can't confuse the two or you've set your mentee up for disappointment or—worse—failure.

Learn Your Mentee's Genius (and Resist Shaping Them into Yours)

I have a dear friend who was my key mentor during my late twenties and into my forties. Let's call him William. He was very successful—in all areas of his life. And he had multiple children, the youngest of whom was his namesake. Same first and last name legally but socially referred to as Bill. (I'm obviously using false names here.) Bill was a delightful kid and brimmed with talent across sports, school, relationships, and the like. But candidly, Bill did not launch so well in his teens. In fact, he faced continued substance abuse challenges, social failures, legal prosecutions, and incarcerations (for year-long stretches) and has multiple children from multiple partners. Huge potential . . . yet unrealized.

From an outside perspective, but with close proximity, I came to see that much of Bill's issues stemmed from trying to be his father. And when he couldn't rise to the level of his father's well-earned success, he would impersonate him. Literally. Write checks against his father's account and steal money. Use his credit cards. Illegally impersonate his father because he shared the same name. Well into his thirties, Bill was still fleecing his father (helped by William's own denial and excuses that many of us desperate parents call love). The epiphany for me was how profoundly destructive it can be when someone compares themselves too critically to someone else. For some, such comparisons can be inspirational and empowering. But for others, the feeling of "not living up" can be demoralizing and devastating. In Bill's case, he faked it and failed miserably.

As a mentor, you must never tempt or allow your mentee to become you, and you may need to look for signs that this is happening. Don't dismiss this suggestion too easily—it happens! So, to avoid this comparison conundrum that can undo all your good mentoring intentions, you must assess your listening skills and work to improve them. I can't help but wonder, had the father listened more intently to his son's passions, fears, feelings, and innate genius, could he have done a better job of both validating and igniting them so the son could feel confident in his own journey? I know I'm likely oversimplifying this as a parent myself, but it's certainly giving me something to ponder as I raise my own three sons and hopefully serve as one of their mentors in life.

Listen and Absorb as an Active Listener

It takes a balance of both desire and skill to employ active listening—to get out of your own head as you construct how you're going to respond or even resist putting into place a well-structured rebuttal. Remember the adage from Dr. Stephen R. Covey, author of *The 7 Habits of Highly Effective People,* "Most people do not listen with the intent to understand; they listen with the intent to reply."

Adopting The Absorber role means you're like a sponge, soaking up everything your mentee feels safe to appropriately share. They indeed have valuable insights you need to understand as a mentor, so The Absorber will ask open-ended, strategic, and thoughtful questions aimed at uncovering so they can discover (see The Revealer). Later in your sessions you might change this formula based on the dynamic, trust, speed, and progress of your interactions, but for your first few sessions follow the 20-80 formula (20 percent talking and 80 percent listening). As you are in listening mode, focus on trying to learn the following:

- What is your mentee trying to accomplish?
- Why?
- By when?
- What was their decision-making process to arrive at their goal?
- What obstacles have they faced so far? How have other attempts gone?
- How will they know when they've succeeded?

Additionally, here are some considerations for you as the mentor to determine how well you've listened to understand:

- Has my mentee articulated a well-defined, accomplishable goal? FranklinCovey teaches the goal-setting formula:

  - From X to Y by When.
  - From _____ to _____ by _____.

- What's my opinion about that goal(s) or lack thereof? Should my opinion even matter?
- What is my mentee's mindset about themselves? Am I uncovering (and thus they are discovering) issues with their self-esteem, self-confidence, education, self-awareness, and professional skill sets that are inhibiting or could accelerate progress toward their goals?

- Am I listening to truly understand how much they believe in themselves? Their confidence and conviction in their goals?
- Am I staying silent until the mentee has finished talking?
- Am I listening with more than my ears by listening with my eyes and heart as well?
- When I do ask questions during my 20 percent allowance, am I doing the following:

  - Checking for understanding (positive)?
  - Finding an opening to change topics (negative)?
  - Surfacing the "burning" issues that are important, critical, or urgent as I perceive them (positive/negative)?
  - Interrupting as a pretext to offer advice (negative)?
  - Repeating back to them what I heard (positive)?

Add to this list, but if you can't readily answer these and other pertinent questions from your mentoring interactions, it's likely you haven't allowed your mentee to do most of the talking, asked the right open-ended questions, or employed active listening.

Practice Intentional Focus and Empathic Listening

True, empathic listening is very difficult, especially as we get ambushed with new information and distractions on a daily, if not hourly, or even minute-by-minute basis. *Focus* has become a leadership and professional competency as a result. So much so that I recently bought a fancy digital egg timer that I carry everywhere with me in my left pocket and use dozens of times a day to focus me in fifteen-minute bursts. Yes, I know there are apps for this sort of thing, but let a guy carry an egg timer around if he wants to! I use it to create dedicated and focused time for phone calls, blog posts, meetings, errands, writing chapters in this book, and the like. I've found that if I can just focus for a mere fifteen minutes on a particular task, my output at the end of the day is shockingly, exponentially higher. As a mentor, you may need to recognize your own challenges with focus, as it absolutely impacts your absorption and listening skills. ADD/ADHD is still a medical diagnosis, but I think everyone in today's world is experiencing some level of attention deficit. And a way to mitigate it is to know your own limitations. You can't be a good listener and Absorber if you're distracted—and let's face it, who's not easily distracted anymore? I recently read that the human attention span is in fact shorter than a goldfish's. My point in addressing focus in The Absorber role is that perhaps you, too, might need to set some parameters about how long a particular topic is discussed, or even the length of your entire mentoring calls and the time of day they're scheduled (see The Boundary Setter, role #2). Maybe you even choose to introduce a timer for certain topics both to ensure focus and prevent the temptation to meander.

What about relationships? Can a mere fifteen minutes of focused attention create positive outcomes for mentors? Absolutely, and this is something The Absorber instinctively knows. The temptation to "fake" listen as our fingers drift with Pavlovian efficiency to answer the "ding" of an incoming text is persistent and compelling. The

Absorber pushes such impulses aside as they focus on their mentee. They fully check in physically, mentally, and emotionally. To that point, great Absorbers intentionally create their physical environment to ensure they've minimized distractions. Take steps to guard against such distractions during your sessions. Consider physically placing yourself where you're least likely to be interrupted or found. (I find sitting in my car, often in the driveway, can be a sanctuary for these types of calls.) Eliminating or at least minimizing potential distractions will certainly help with your focus and have a positive impact on your ability to listen.

Another important consideration to maximize your role as The Absorber is to better understand your own natural listening style. For many of us in our careers, we've had an assessment of our personality style, our leadership style, and even our communication style. But when have you ever thought about your listening style? Dr. Stephen R. Covey offered that our listening styles tend to congeal around four techniques: probing, interpreting, advising, and evaluating. Take a few moments and review those four words. Which might best describe how you "pretend listen"? And maybe this is an intelligence test now, but none of them are helpful in mentoring—at least not when you're in The Absorber role.

Instead of these four styles that tend to culminate in what's known as pretend listening, focus more on empathic listening. Do you understand what your mentee is saying, feeling, struggling with? Are you capable of trying to walk in their shoes? And remember not to confuse empathy with sympathy. Your key goal as an empathic listener is understanding. Why do they feel this way? Why do they think that? Why do they believe that?

Keep in mind, you can validate someone without agreeing with them (see The Validator, role #6).

Empathic listening is a skill that comes only with practice. Focused, repeated practice. It's not easy, so give yourself some forgiveness. But as long as your intent is to understand, you're going to make improvements and they will be felt by your mentee (and bonus, your spouse/partner).

Stop Interrupting

If you find yourself to be an "interrupter"—and news flash, most of us are—you might consider some tactical reminders to stop speaking. Practice and implement the somewhat funny but very practical advice from Dr. Deborah Tannen, the renowned linguistics and communications author and Georgetown University professor. Dr. Tannen reminds us that the main reason we interrupt others is because we possess what she calls "an internal, silent alarm clock" that goes off in our heads when we think the other person should stop talking.

Comical.

Simple.

Profound.

When we think another person should stop talking, we interject and interrupt to accomplish one of several objectives:

- Simply stop them from talking—otherwise to just shut them up
- Intend to solve a problem that you see and feel they don't

- Try to speed them along, hoping they'll finally land their point
- Hope they see the genius and wisdom in your inserted contribution and go act on it

Interrupting is a very natural communication style for many of us. Horrifyingly so, as it has become commonplace in our increasingly rushed conversations.

Here's a great tip to consider if you acknowledge you're an interrupter (and thus a poor and impatient listener). The next time you're in a conversation and you're tempted to insert your point of view . . . simply don't. Close your lips.

Gently.

Carefully.

Slowly.

And ensure your upper lip and lower lip touch each other (without grimacing or any visibly physical effort). With your lips closed, with neither a frown nor smile, count to ten—or longer—until the urge to interject your point passes. (For the record, with this advice, I've just vastly improved your marriage or relationship with a partner.)

Dr. Tannen's research shows that if you can resist interrupting, it's during these ten-second time periods (sometimes shorter, sometimes longer), that the odds the speaker (mentee) will do one of several things raises significantly:

- They will simply conclude by landing their key point sooner than you expected.
- They will somehow invite you into the conversation.

- They will indicate how they would like you to respond.

I highly recommend you reread this section as many times as is necessary to integrate it into your own communication and listening style—it's life changing.

Be Gentle on Yourself and Know When to Be Prescriptive

Be gentle and forgiving of yourself for what will inevitably be a continued set of challenges you face on your journey to become The Absorber: A wandering mind. An interruption. A self-serving question. A lack of empathy. A subconscious hidden agenda. A curious mind run amok.

It happens. Frequently. Every few minutes for most of us.

The key is to know when these temptations are creeping into your mentoring style and try to minimize them. The good news is, the more you practice these insights, the more instinctive they will become.

Of course, at some point The Absorber has done their job and it's time to offer solutions, paths, ideas, and strategies to help their mentee achieve success. And much of that is an outcome of asking great questions, exactly the competency found in the next mentor role, The Questioner (role #4).

Captures—Additional Tools

PRE-MENTORING REFLECTION

Consider those who have played The Absorber role in your life (this might include formal mentors, colleagues, parents, friends, teachers, and ecclesiastical leaders). Review which of the Key Absorber Skills illustrated in the chapter opening that they demonstrated and describe the impact in your life:

_____

_____

_____

_____

Capture the "big ideas" you have about The Absorber role. Consider your own mentoring experiences. What in life has prepared you for this role? What might you need to do to prepare more? What can you adopt from the previous exercise? Write your thoughts below:

_____

_____

_____

_____

_____

IN-THE-MOMENT MENTORING PROMPTS

Revisit the questions and key insights found throughout The Absorber chapter. These could include both questions for the mentee or reflection questions to help you with your mentoring mindset. Chose which feel the most relevant to an upcoming mentoring session and write them below. If the questions are reflective in nature, take a moment to answer them for yourself.

Mentee Questions

Question 1:

_____

Question 2:

_____

Role 3: The Absorber

Question 3:

_____

Question 4:

_____

Mentor Reflection Questions

Question 1:

_____

Answer:

_____

Question 2:

_____

Answer:

_____

Question 3:

_____

Answer:

_____

Question 4:

_____

Answer:

_____

POST-MENTORING LEARNING

Following your mentoring session, think back to how things went when adopting The Absorber role. Some roles may feel more natural to you than others, but they all benefit from objectively assessing what worked, what didn't, and what you can learn as a result.

1. *Circle the answer that best corresponds to this statement:* "The Absorber role was effective for me as a mentor during the mentoring session."

    a. Strongly agree
    b. Agree
    c. Neutral
    d. Disagree
    e. Strongly disagree

2. *Circle the answer that best corresponds to this statement:* "In the mentoring session, I achieved the Absorber goal: 'To invest your focused time and attention into your mentee through active listening, empathy, and intentional focus.'"

    a. Strongly agree
    b. Agree
    c. Neutral
    d. Disagree
    e. Strongly disagree

3. **Explore the "why" behind your answers.** Consider what worked and didn't in your mentoring session. What should you stop or start doing? What might you do less or more of? If you found gaps in your ability to execute this role, what can you do to close them? Capture your learning from this session and anything that, on reflection, could help you grow to be more comfortable and capable in this role:

_____

_____

_____

_____

_____

Role 4:
The Questioner

The Questioner works like a skilled attorney—less like a prosecuting attorney but more like a defense attorney. Often, a prosecuting attorney puts the accused on the "stand" and badgers them into submission, resulting in feelings of guilt, confusion, and worthlessness—all in an attempt to extract a confession. This is their job. The defense attorney, ideally, relies more on their empathic skills, relatability, common experience, and insight to help zero in on the right issue to exonerate their client. I warned you earlier in this book that I would use a lot of metaphors—sometimes they work well and sometimes they don't. The jury may be out on this one, but I think you get my point: You want to stay far from weaponizing your questions against your mentee. The Questioner is adept at employing insightful questioning and identifying and catching problems early by asking the right questions at the right time, in the right way, and with the right intent.

The Goal

Use thoughtful, relevant, and open-ended questions to help the mentee zero in on the right root cause or underlying issue that can then be worked through together.

The Upside When The Questioner Role Is Employed Well

- Reduces risks by catching critical issues early
- Builds trust by making "bad" news safe to discuss
- Helps the mentee focus on the right things at the right times
- Uncovers insecurities and misconceptions that might be getting in their way
- Surfaces other issues that may need to be addressed

The Downside When The Questioner Role Is Abdicated

When the mentor is asking self-serving or extraneous questions based on their own agenda, experience, and timeline, the mentee can be forced into offering responses or "solutions" that have little to do with what they ultimately want to accomplish in order to satisfy the mentor's needs.

Key Questioner Skills

- Employ a laser-like focus to cut through confusion and create clarity
- Recognize that "right" is what progresses your mentee's goal
- Make it safe to share bad or embarrassing news
- Guard against the "wrong" news
- Build trust and establish safety
- Avoid prosecutorial badgering
- Effectively employ "early-" and "later-" stage questions

This role likely will come naturally to you.

Perhaps too naturally. Like all strengths in life, when overplayed they can become liabilities. So it's important to calibrate your questioning skills to get to the root cause as efficiently as possible without compromising a safe environment for your mentee.

As a reminder, my assumption for most mentors is that they hail from well-established careers with some level of longevity. If that premise is correct, then it's also reasonable that most mentors have a useful set of acquired business and leadership skills handy when working with their mentees, including the skill of asking piercingly insightful and even penetrating questions. This may work well when getting to the bottom line of organizational issues around margin or profitability, but less well when trying to uncover someone's personal passions and professional career goals. A common skill leaders employ, and consequently in their role as mentor, is the ability to get to the root cause of an issue quickly and accurately, also called "peeling the onion." Again, it can be an asset or a liability depending upon the situation, circumstance, and goal of the relationship. Just proceed with caution and be certain to employ this once the right level of trust has been built with your mentee. Remember your mentee is not your employee (or prosecutorial witness on the stand).

Employ a Laser-Like Focus to Cut Through Confusion and Create Clarity

Don't for a moment think that I don't value the skill of asking penetrating questions. It can be a differentiating asset to leaders and mentors alike. The key is just knowing when and how to employ it with your mentee. In the television game show *Name That Tune*, contestants tried to name a song in as few notes as possible. Conversely, The Questioner draws on their intuition, knowledge, expertise, and other "clues"—aka observable data—to identify the right underlying issue and make it actionable (more on "rightness" in the next section). Efficiency isn't always effective when employing The Questioner role.

Over the course of my leadership experience, I can usually identify "the bottom line" in fewer than four questions. Sometimes in just one with the right level of eye contact and precision in my diction. Helpful? Sure, if you're the parent of three young sons. Or a federal prosecutor or personal injury attorney working solely on contingency. Time is money in business, and the skill of asking penetrating questions can quickly eliminate confusion and create clarity. So, it's vital to differentiate between your capacity to ask questions in your leadership role versus your capacity to ask questions in your mentoring role. Your charge as a mentor is to employ the wisdom to know the difference. Remember, how you ask questions can be both an asset and a liability depending on your role and the circumstance.

Recognize That "Right" Is What Progresses Your Mentee's Goal

The Questioner understands there is a "right" answer to be found, when "right" is determined by how the issue connects and accelerates success toward the mentees' stated goal. This is a delicate process mentors need to model to keep their mentee focused and not meander too far into adjacent topics, experiences, or even personal traumas. So it may be that your job is to put some boundaries on *yourself* and limit the types of questions you ask to ensure you and your mentee are focused on getting to the right "right." This is tricky. What's "right" may change over the course of your time together. What seems "right" to you may seem wrong to your mentee. Tread carefully here, recognizing it may not always be a black or white discussion, and the more comfortability you demonstrate in the gray can empower your mentee to continue thinking about their various options. We all know that in life "right" usually can't be forced, but in the scope of the mentoring relationship, the litmus test for "right" is almost certainly found in whether you are advancing clarity around how it supports their stated goal.

Make It Safe to Share Bad or Embarrassing News

Personally, I relish asking and being asked uncomfortable questions, as it simply ups the game of everyone involved. One of my own adages I've drilled into everyone who's ever worked for me goes like this:

"*Bad* news is acceptable. *Wrong* news is unacceptable."

Any leader, owner, or entrepreneur understands bad news is inevitable: Pricing was misquoted, shipments were delayed, deals were lost, revenue failed to materialize . . . It's endless. The Questioner relies on building the trust and safety necessary to be told the truth. I've learned over the years the faster I can get to the "bad news," the faster and easier it is for me to help them solve it, collaboratively find a workaround, or independently move to plan B—which I always, *always* have. And a plan C, D, and E. This isn't a case of setting cultural permission to fall short on commitments so that the leader/mentor is invited or forced to solve the issue, command and control style. But rather, to create a culture of trust where it's safe to share bad news early enough to do something constructively about it.

Conversely, if I'm feared for my temper, retaliatory nature, or propensity to embarrass or belittle my team, people will withhold the bad news no matter how focused my questions are. That's followed by the mentee going off to attempt to solve the *whatever-it-was-it-was-so-bad-they-were-afraid-to-tell-me* problem on their own. Soon they're fatigued as they exhaust their creativity and skills and are forced to come back, hat in hand, and have the discussion we should have had much earlier.

To be clear, The Questioner wants bad news. Frequently and early. For me, the receipt of bad news doesn't always mean I'm going to solve the problem for you, or I'm going to give you a pass on your commitments and deliverables. But here's the irony: Sharing bad news builds trust. And as that trust increases, it will become your competitive advantage . . . something called transparency. And transparency is what the best cultures, organizations, and mentor-mentee relationships all have in common. To summarize, as a mentor, you need to make it safe for your mentee to share bad and embarrassing news. *You* create the conditions for this to be easy—or hard. Not them.

Guard Against the "Wrong" News

Now let's talk about wrong news.

The Questioner understands that wrong news is simply not acceptable and communicates this to their mentee. Wrong news comes in the form of misinformation, warped perceptions, factually untrue statements, and sometimes lies.

Wrong news shows the mentee may be doing the following:

- Lying or fabricating facts and hoping they won't be found out (likely because of a lack of trust and/or safety with their mentor)
- Risking highlighting their incompetence (conscious or otherwise) and requires coaching and mentorship beyond solving the problem at hand
- Operating with misinformation about key facts and needs the perspective and insights of the mentor to help them reorient to what's really going on

Now these may seem far-fetched in a mentoring situation and more suited to a professional leader-subordinate relationship, but you should be prepared for anything coming your way.

The Questioner must put aside their ego to be effective. Their exploration with their mentee is not about inflating their own hubris—the very thing that may have prevented them from asking the right questions in the first place. The Questioner isn't looking to be the soloist or the hero—stepping in front of the orchestra to take the spotlight or swooping in to save the day. Instead, they're focused on quickly getting to clarity—around the issue, the desired outcomes, and the way forward. The Questioner often asks the boldest questions, as trust is established early in the mentoring relationship when they have plenty of runway to work with.

If a mentee is delivering "wrong news," conscious or not, that's an indicator you may need to create a safer environment for them to acknowledge their disconnection with facts and logic. By asking the right questions at the right time, wrong news *can* be nearly eliminated—and really, that's the goal. The impact a mentor can have in this situation can be incalculable. A mentee stuck delivering wrong news will muddle through their professional lives and stay frustrated with their lack of relevance and control over their future. We've all seen these cul-de-sac careers in people.

Build Trust and Establish Safety

The Questioner is only as effective as the amount of trust they've built with their mentee. They make it safe for the mentee to say something that might seem elementary or to risk judgment. Perhaps you remind your mentee that in most professional settings, the boss appreciates rudimentary questions because they always lead to greater clarity and vision lock.

The Questioner can aim for efficiency, but only if they adopt this role without making it their default style. They also know that it is always worth it to take "six more minutes" in a meeting to ensure their mentee is 100 percent aligned with what success looks like.

Think about The Questioner as you would a skilled courtroom attorney. No doubt the attorney will ask precise questions as they "peel the onion" and get to the important points of their argument. But of course they've met with their client and have gone over all the important issues beforehand. So similarly, it might be valuable when you plan to be in The Questioner role to communicate some of the things you think would be helpful to address beforehand, so your mentee is not caught off guard in the moment. This could be via email, Slack message, text, or the calendar appointment itself, so that the mentee has a chance to think through their answers and position, while simultaneously minimizing the chance they feel backed into a corner, in real time. So, The Questioner is like a defense attorney in some ways but definitely *not* in others (as you'll see in the next section).

Avoid Prosecutorial Badgering

Forming the "right" questions in the workplace is not a directly transferable skill to mentoring. You may well have earned a meta-phorical PhD in business interrogations but that can be easily wea-ponized against your mentee. If you've played The Revealer (role #1) well, you've entered the mentoring site gently and carefully and hold the mindset to uncover to discover. Mentoring is not the time to demonstrate your prosecutorial skills by pummeling your mentee with piercing and invasive tirades. You may very well want to lead *that* discussion with your professional team, uncovering why they're missing their revenue/profit commitments and how you're supposed to defend/explain that to the analysts and investors. Great skill, wrong setting.

As a mentor, the role of The Questioner should be graduated in correlation with your rapport, trust, and even developing friendship. However, the further along you are in your relationship, the more penetrating and even frightening your questions can be (more on that in a bit). Early on, you want to focus on big, bold, open-ended questions—not the "yes or no" kind of stuff a skilled prosecutor uses to paint a defendant into a corner.

Effectively Employ "Early-" and "Later-" Stage Questions

The Questioner asks directional questions based on the maturity of the relationship. Here is a list of candidates you might consider early on, followed by more specific questions you may ask as you've set some relationship expectations (and boundaries) and your mutual personalities are understood and appreciated. Remember, piercing questions that challenge your mentee are invaluable *when well-timed*.

EARLY-PHASE QUESTIONS

- Tell me about your journey in life. Maybe a few minutes personally and then a few minutes professionally. Perhaps share some milestones that you think would be important for me to know about.

- Tell me about a person you admire and why. Be specific. What about their life would you like to emulate?
- How do you define success?

  - *(Be sure to clarify that you have no judgment on what they say, you just want to better understand what matters to them and how they would measure that.)*

- What do you see as your strengths? Weaknesses? Areas of improvement worth investing in?

  - *(Perhaps state you never plan to be a chemist, so memorizing the periodic table of elements likely isn't the best use of your time. Remember, make it safe for your mentee to tell you their truth.)*

- Have you identified your personal and professional values? What's most important to you?

  - *(Clarify that they are indeed different. Someone's religious faith or freedom of speech might be an important personal value while maximizing their income or landing an international assignment might be a professional value. You should have your own well-thought-through values at the ready, in case they struggle and ask for some examples.)*

- What types of roles, assignments, projects, teams, goals invigorate you? Crush you? Bore you? Stifle you?
- What do you dream about accomplishing?

- What fears do you have that you've told no one about?

  - *(Reinforce that some may even be irrational. Again—be ready to share some of your own.)*

- Do you ever feel like an impostor? When? Why? How could we minimize that?
- What inspires and motivates you?
- What are you hoping will come from our time together over the coming [time frame]?
- Are there any specific expectations you have of me that might be helpful for me to know?
- What would you like to know about my journey that could better empower you to leverage our time together?
- Is there anything you'd like me to know about your personality or communication style that might maximize our flow together?

LATER-PHASE QUESTIONS

- I notice a word you use frequently is [word]; why is that word so easy for you to use?
- I recognize you seem to talk overly [positively/negatively/diminishingly/self-promotionally] about yourself. How is that working/not working for you?
- I seem to see a lot of focus on [others/your boss/your parents/your partner/your nemesis/your idol]. Can we talk about how that's helping/not helping you achieve your goals?

- Can I share an observation about something I see coming up frequently in your language and examples? (It may be positive or negative.) Can we explore why that's so present in your mind?
- Can I opine on some common themes I see you revisiting and what I think you might want to consider?
- We're [X] percent through our time together, is there a focused area you wish we were perhaps more disciplined in addressing?
- Is there anything about my style that is contributing to your ability/inability to achieve the success we've co-defined for you?

These questions will often require empathy and patience and may surface a surprising or dominating underlying belief. It may then be necessary to ask questions such as these:

- Can you tell me more about this belief of yours?
- Can you share any specific experiences you've been through that have proven this to be correct?
- Can you tell me, was there someone specific in your life who taught you this belief or encouraged you to follow this line of thinking?

Depending on their answer or what they disclose, you may need to switch to The Validator (role #6) to affirm their thoughts and feelings. And if you'd like to challenge those beliefs and push on their established paradigm, you may need to move to The Challenger (role #5). Depending on the trust you've built with your mentee, you might share an outdated belief you once held, that was indoctrinated into you, and later in life you learned wasn't entirely true. This type of self-disclosure can be exactly what's needed to set the conditions, environment, and culture of your sessions so that the mentee feels safe in a space of vulnerability. The Questioner is always on the lookout and ready to nimbly switch to another role if the answers to their questions warrant it.

The Questioner Role and Me

I was once standing outside my CEO's office waiting for a meeting when his door opened and a young man in his late teens or early twenties exited. This young gentleman was not an employee of the company but appeared to be ending a conversation about some relationship he had with the CEO personally. Maybe a neighbor, church member, or some other role where the CEO appeared to have been coaching him. As the gentleman walked out of the doorway, I overheard the CEO say with equal parts graciousness and sternness, "Well, I guess if you're not going to do what you said you would, then there's nothing left for us to talk about."

I know this CEO well enough to know that one of his key competencies was asking strategic and even piercingly insightful questions of all those he meets with—employees or otherwise. But even the most illuminating questions can't guarantee someone is going to deliver on their commitments. Therefore, in certain situations, you may have to ask yourself, "Have my questions been effective at setting my mentee up to make and keep commitments to themselves and me?" Many of us tend to ask questions that are rooted in our own frame of reference or what we feel we need to know, when in fact we may benefit from challenging our natural question-asking abilities to ensure they're aimed at helping our mentee find an answer that strengthens their ability to deliver on a commitment.

Sometimes in a mentoring relationship, the questions we've been asking have either run their course or simply aren't driving our mentee toward any level of accountability or behavior change. You may need to consider if the questions you're asking are driving the right introspection and even mentee commitment. If not, simply asking more questions may not be the solution and it may be time to employ a different role.

Captures—Additional Tools

PRE-MENTORING REFLECTION

Consider those who have played The Questioner role in your life (this might include formal mentors, colleagues, parents, friends, teachers, and ecclesiastical leaders). Review which of the Key Questioner Skills illustrated in the chapter opening that they demonstrated and describe the impact in your life:

_____

_____

_____

_____

_____

Role 4: The Questioner

Capture the "big ideas" you have about The Questioner role. Consider your own mentoring experiences. What in life has prepared you for this role? What might you need to do to prepare more? What can you adopt from the previous exercise? Write your thoughts below:

_____

_____

_____

_____

_____

IN-THE-MOMENT MENTORING PROMPTS

Revisit the questions and key insights found throughout The Questioner chapter. These could include both questions for the mentee or reflection questions to help you with your mentoring mindset. Choose which feel the most relevant to an upcoming mentoring session and write them below. If the questions are reflective in nature, take a moment to answer them for yourself.

Mentee Questions

Question 1:

_____

Question 2:

_____

Question 3:

_____

Question 4:

_____

Mentor Reflection Questions

Question 1:

_____

Answer:

_____

Question 2:

_____

Answer:

_____

Question 3:

_____

Answer:

_____

Question 4:

_____

Answer:

_____

POST-MENTORING LEARNING

Following your mentoring session, think back to how things went when adopting The Questioner role. Some roles may feel more natural to you than others, but they all benefit from objectively assessing what worked, what didn't, and what you can learn as a result.

1. *Circle the answer that best corresponds to this statement:* "The Questioner role was effective for me as a mentor during the mentoring session."

    a. Strongly agree
    b. Agree
    c. Neutral
    d. Disagree
    e. Strongly disagree

2. *Circle the answer that best corresponds to this statement:* "In the mentoring session, I achieved The Questioner goal: 'Use thoughtful, relevant, and open-ended questions to help the mentee zero in on the right root cause or underlying issue that can then be worked through together.'"

    a. Strongly agree
    b. Agree
    c. Neutral
    d. Disagree
    e. Strongly disagree

3. **Explore the "why" behind your answers.** Consider what worked and didn't in your mentoring session. What should you stop or start doing? What might you do less or more of? If you found gaps in your ability to execute this role, what can you do to close them? Capture your learning from this session and anything that, on reflection, could help you grow more comfortable and capable in this role:

_____

_____

_____

_____

_____

Role 5:
The Challenger

The Challenger tactfully pushes their mentee to confront assumptions, perspectives, mindsets, or behaviors that are impeding their performance. They determine the level of confrontation that will be helpful given the mentee and the situation, parsing facts from feelings as they model the critical thinking that will serve the mentee throughout their professional life.

The Goal

Use challenges to prompt critical analysis so mentees are more introspective and use sound reasoning in their decision-making.

. . .

The Upside When The Challenger Role Is Employed Well

- Provides additional clarity for both the mentor and mentee
- Surfaces bias, misunderstandings, faulty assumptions, flawed perspectives, and errant information
- Separates feelings from facts
- Assumes the "right" intervention is not simply what worked for the mentor in the past
- Teaches the mentee to employ critical thinking and challenge their own suppositions before taking action

The Downside When The Challenger Role Is Abdicated

Without the due diligence of critical analysis, mentees are left to execute against untested assumptions and flawed perspectives, wasting time, energy, and separating them even further from achieving the goals that matter most to them.

Key Challenger Skills

- Know *when* to challenge
- Ensure your mindset is focused on the mentee's goals and skills (not yours)
- Allow the mentee space to share

- Separate feelings from facts
- Assess your natural style on The Challenger Continuum
- Plot the right challenge level

A colleague of mine calls the best mentoring situational. Meaning that great mentors are fiercely focused on understanding and helping their mentee determine which skills, goals, and experiences they're eager to accomplish and how to create a path to achieve them. And these paths are different in every mentoring situation.

Not an epiphany, I know, but I intend to restate it throughout this book. As a mentor, it can be dangerously tempting to force your mentee into your formula for success based on your own career trajectory. For some mentors, it might become tempting to merely accept whatever goal a mentee offers, assuming they've thought through *their* goals, skills, and motivations adequately. Both scenarios can be a disaster. And so, The Challenger "pushes back"—throwing the metaphorical switch on even the most carefully laid tracks and offering an alternative when appropriate.

Know *When* to Challenge

The Challenger role is about pushing on anything and everything if you think it will help your mentee. OK, not literally "anything and everything," as that might seriously damage their sense of self-esteem and, candidly, would be fatiguing for anyone. There is a time and place for validation (in fact The Validator [role #6] is coming next), but The Challenger has a different job to do. Consider situations where The Challenger role is especially helpful:

- An underlying assumption or belief (likely surfaced by The Questioner, role #4) is drastically misaligned with the mentee's goals.
- The mentee has a warped sense of "reality" and an accompanying unhealthy mindset.
- There's a disconnect between perspectives, reactions, and "facts" that warrants further introspection and/or reconnecting with governing principles.
- The mentee has decided something too quickly and would benefit from slowing down and validating their assumptions and/or reasoning.
- The mentee seems to be saying something you think they heard but may not truly believe.
- Rather than announcing that something is simply "wrong," the mentor wants to push just enough for the mentee to figure it out on their own (and thus build the capacity to do this in the future).
- Your mentee is delusional (sorry, but it can happen). Perhaps their view of reality is radically off, or their assessment of their skills and abilities is wildly unrealistic. They are otherwise rational when it comes to their work, but they've been in a personal relationship or professional setting where the negative situation colors everything they see.

Be careful as The Challenger that you're not engaged in an exercise to minimize the pain from a previous experience, setback, violation, or failure. As The Challenger, you may interpret the mentee's boundaries, resulting from such experiences, as too tight and even restricting growth. Don't fall into the trap of saying, "Well that's rough, but at least [X] didn't happen." As taught in The Validator role, you can affirm someone's experience without agreeing with their conclusions.

It's important to note here, if serious violations are present, you are likely not qualified to push on them and should tread lightly. Validate their pain, concerns, or boundaries and move to other opportunities for growth.

Ensure Your Mindset Is Focused on the Mentee's Goals and Skills (Not Yours)

As I reflect on the many people I've mentored as a leader, too many of them are following paths I envisioned based on what I would have done if I were them (and not if they were them): things like write a column, create a blog, author a book, design a course, perfect a keynote presentation, build a social media platform, or assemble a card deck and sell it online. These are things I do—candidly, quite well—in pursuit of the goals I have, drawing on the talents I possess. (Too many I's . . . ? Yep.)

Which is exactly the problem. Sometimes you may need to employ The Challenger role on *yourself.* Rarely will a mentee have the same goals, skills, and motivations as their mentor (nor will a predefined formula for success, burned into a leader's psyche after years of use, necessarily be the "right" solution for them). Do not dismiss my somewhat pedantic repeating of this watch-out, because it creeps into every mentoring mindset and role. You need to use great discretion when something you've done is also something your mentee should or shouldn't do. Being able to challenge yourself demonstrates you're growing as a result of your mentoring investment.

Allow the Mentee Space to Share

Because a challenge can feel threatening, even when handled carefully, make sure you've given the mentee plenty of space to explore and share. A great phrase to use is "Thanks for sharing that; it was very valuable for me. Is that a complete download, or are there any other facts or opinions you'd like to share that might help me better understand?"

Then pause.

Take a breath.

Follow up with statements like the following:

- "Thanks for sharing more with me. That's very helpful."
- "Could you further define what you mean when you say [X]?"
- "You mentioned [Y]. Could you give me a real-life example of that?"
- "Is what you shared something you have firsthand knowledge about, or something you *believe* to be the case?"
- "As I listened to what you shared, I think it's important for me to clarify a few points . . ."

  - "Did you mean to say [Y]?"
  - "When you said [X], I understood you to mean that [Z] was happening. Do I have that right, or have I

misunderstood you—because what I'm hearing is very different from my own experience and what my intuition is telling me."

This is certainly not an exhaustive list of challenge prompts. But it should give you a sense of what The Challenger is trying to accomplish: to validate what the mentee *purports* to be true as *actually* being true.

Separate Feelings from Facts

The Challenger ensures that the mentee owns the words they use, their meaning, and their mindset. When in The Challenger role, remind your mentee that it's human nature to confuse and conflate feelings with facts. Both are important, but feelings are feelings and facts are facts and they're very different. When you're in The Challenger role, you're likely more concerned with the world of facts and may take on The Questioner (role #4) to unearth them (being careful not to back your mentee into a corner or put them on the defensive). Depending on what such questions bring to life, The Challenger may be called on to test or dispute what was learned.

Assess Your Natural Style on The Challenger Continuum

Before I introduce The Challenger Continuum, you'll need to exercise some self-awareness over what your natural style is regarding how you challenge others:

- Are you aggressive by nature and challenging is easy and feels automatic? (My wife, Stephanie, insists I'm so comfortable with conflict that I seek it out—to which I'm happy to explain how wrong she is, in great detail, while relishing the thought of my eventual [hopeful] victory as we argue about it late into the evening.)
- Do you avoid conflict at all costs? (There are experienced, successful leaders and mentors who become physically ill at the thought of a disagreement and have mastered changing the subject, excusing themselves with a call or restroom visit, or slipping out the back exit and making a run for cover.)
- And then there is everyone in between.

You need to confront your natural style and become introspective about how it works both for and against you—and for or against others—as you take on The Challenger role. But don't back off on the required courage to step outside your comfort zone. We've all benefited from someone who challenged us and pushed on our beliefs about ourselves. Such mentors can become Transition Figures—those who disrupt a rote narrative and truly challenge a mentee to confront a repeated limiting belief about themselves or self-defeating behaviors. Such a mentor actually *transitions* them into a new mindset, a new reality, a new life.

Plot the Right Challenge Level

When you've deemed yourself sufficiently self-aware (let's face it, you're unlikely to change your *personality* much at this point in life, so self-awareness and mild mitigation is your best bet to building relationships), you can now put The Challenger Continuum to use. Plot both where you currently are and where you want to be, given your mentee and their set of unique circumstances.

Low Challenge

Abdicating your role as a mentor because you're focused on feelings and not progress. Shame on you.

Obfuscating or "Beating around the bush." Providing hint bombs, hoping they drop and explode while you run the other way.

Suggesting confusion or equivocation but not outright stating your issue for fear of upsetting them or being asked for an alternative.

Deliberately deciding this is/is not a battle you want to take on. (Is the consequence of challenging going to pay off . . . for them and you?)

Challenging through respectful clarity. I'd call this The Questioner's "peeling the onion" skill to ensure you understand the mentee's statement so you can respond.

A clear challenge, but with inquisitive rather than exclamatory language (likely formed as a question).

Clear, firm word choice with unequivocal language and tone that stops momentum in its tracks.

Aggressive and dominating with no room for negotiation. Scorched earth approach. (Good luck with this.)

High Challenge

The Challenger Role and Me

I once worked with a technically competent, executive-level associate who had a default challenge phrase: "I'm not interested in that." It was their attempt to shut down the shit they didn't like, support, agree with, relate to, or perhaps even intellectually or emotionally understand. They said this so often it rang in my ears like the '80s sitcom tagline: "Whatcha talkin' bout, Willis?" Under fifty? Google it.

This phrase was their go-to challenge to ensure the other person (often me) didn't see any invitation to progress. It was done. Dead on arrival. Next topic, idiot.

This was, for them, a masterful pivot tactic that worked. But sadly, their influence waned and relationships throughout the organization suffered—for other reasons as well. I've been on both the delivering and receiving side of this type of challenge. It stings. But not so much as it burns. Or maybe it does both, just without the scarring. Either way, this communication technique is *sometimes* necessary in clarifying expectations, setting boundaries, or providing guardrails for what you're able as a mentor to do and what you can't or won't do (see The Boundary Setter, role #2). When I'm entering a mentoring relationship, I'll often tell my mentee that there will be occasions when they need to "bruise hard and heal fast." Welcome to life.

I recently was mentoring a new, short-lived person (not her life, just our relationship) and during our first and only call, I made a fatal mistake. I said, "I feel on this topic that you're unconsciously incompetent." Meaning *you don't know what you don't know*. But lacking trust and time between us, she was too offended to continue with me.

Shame on her.

Shame on me.

I never should have used a harsh statement like that in an opening call. (I actually think it was a piercingly accurate assessment but, good grief, Scott, thirty minutes into the first call?!)

I like this type of challenge. Sometimes challenging statements can be genuinely expressed as questions. "When you said your boss is totally incompetent, did you really mean they have zero competence at any level? Because in most organizations, that would also mean everyone above them must be incompetent as well to allow that leader to even remain employed." You get the point. Give your mentee a chance to recover or clarify while letting them know hyperbole or generalizations in life are never helpful. Unless you're campaigning for elected office and then, apparently, they're requisite.

Mirroring to someone the exact words they used, without your spin or different word choice, can also be invaluably sobering. "Can I repeat back what I just heard? You said you feel your business plan is solid and ready for presentation to thirty investors, even though you've not illustrated any multiyear revenue projections because they won't care about that. Did I get that right?" Gulp.

Finally, allow me to offer some solid marriage, er, I mean mentoring advice. Choose your confrontation battles wisely. This is a concept I learned early and fast at FranklinCovey: *Do you want to win the battle or win the war?* There's a difference! Plenty of military leaders have won skirmishes and battles but ended up losing the larger war. In business, I've seen this countless times as someone takes an absurdly hard stand on a seemingly arcane issue, but somehow, they must die on their sword rather than tactically retreat. And they do . . . die on their sword. Their influence in the organization plummets (usually due to low self-awareness, low to no self-regulation, and myopic thinking), and while they may win the battle (that singular issue they were strangely, obsessively focused on) it costs them the war (the overall view of their judgment and subsequent reputation). The goal of The Challenger is to win the war—and the "war" is helping your mentee stay focused on and accomplish their expressed goals.

Play The Challenger role when necessary, but don't patronize people. Your mentee's time is just as valuable to them as yours is to you. So if you think challenging their idea/path/logic/vision/rationale/mindset/research is worthy and in service of helping them succeed, then do it—that's what The Challenger role is for. But let's be honest, it takes courage. If that isn't your strength in life, ask, "Can I challenge something you said, as maybe I misunderstood, or perhaps I don't fully understand?"

As a mentor, employing The Challenger role doesn't always equate to you having the answer or being the expert in things like Six Sigma, Capitalization (Cap) Tables, artificial intelligence, lean manufacturing, immigration issues, import/export tariffs, and on and on. You are, however, likely an effective generalist bringing your life's wisdom to the conversation. Don't be hesitant or even afraid to say, "Although I'm challenging you on this topic, I also don't have the answer. But it sounds important/vital/consequential, so let's both go research it a bit more before you go all in."

There is no room for sustained cowardice with The Challenger. Nor is there room for reckless bravado. It's a careful balancing act that the most effective mentors learn to employ well.

Captures—Additional Tools

PRE-MENTORING REFLECTION

Consider those who have played The Challenger role in your life (this might include formal mentors, colleagues, parents, friends, teachers, and ecclesiastical leaders). Review which of the Key Challenger Skills illustrated in the chapter opening that they demonstrated and describe the impact in your life:

_____

_____

_____

_____

Capture the "big ideas" you have about The Challenger role. Consider your own mentoring experiences. What in life has prepared you for this role? What might you need to do to prepare more? What can you adopt from the previous exercise? Write your thoughts below:

_____

_____

_____

_____

_____

IN-THE-MOMENT MENTORING PROMPTS

Revisit the questions and key insights found throughout The Challenger chapter. These could include both questions for the mentee or reflection questions to help you with your mentoring mindset. Choose which feel the most relevant to an upcoming mentoring session and write them below. If the questions are reflective in nature, take a moment to answer them for yourself.

Mentee Questions

Question 1:

_____

Question 2:

_____

Role 5: The Challenger

Question 3:

_____

Question 4:

_____

Mentor Reflection Questions

Question 1:

_____

Answer:

_____

Question 2:

_____

Answer:

_____

Question 3:

_____

Answer:

_____

Question 4:

_____

Answer:

_____

POST-MENTORING LEARNING

Following your mentoring session, think back to how things went when adopting The Challenger role. Some roles may feel more natural to you than others, but they all benefit from objectively assessing what worked, what didn't, and what you can learn as a result.

1. *Circle the answer that best corresponds to this statement:* "The Challenger role was effective for me as a mentor during the mentoring session."

   a. Strongly agree

   b. Agree

   c. Neutral

   d. Disagree

   e. Strongly disagree

2. *Circle the answer that best corresponds to this statement:* "In the mentoring session, I achieved the Challenger goal: 'Use challenges to prompt critical analysis so mentees are more introspective and use sound reasoning in their decision-making.'"

   a. Strongly agree

   b. Agree

   c. Neutral

   d. Disagree

   e. Strongly disagree

3. **Explore the "why" behind your answers.** Consider what worked and didn't in your mentoring session. What should you stop or start doing? What might you do less or more of? If you found gaps in your ability to execute this role, what can you do to close them? Capture your learning from this session and anything that, on reflection, could help you grow to be more comfortable and capable in this role:

_____

_____

_____

_____

_____

Role 6: The Validator

The Validator strengthens the mentoring relationship by recognizing, accepting, and communicating that the internal experience (thoughts, feelings, emotions, perceptions, beliefs) of their mentee, whatever they may be, are valid and worthy. The Validator may not agree with the mentee's conclusions about such experiences, but they recognize you don't have to agree with someone to validate them. The Validator simply wants to affirm their mentee's emotions, state of mind, and ability to accomplish their own expressed goals, while ensuring they feel seen and understood.

The Goal

To strengthen the mentoring relationship and progress their journey by strategically validating a mentee's confidence, competence, fears, and anxieties.

The Upside When The Validator Role Is Employed Well

- Communicates acceptance
- Calms intense emotions so mentoring can be more effective
- Expresses that internal experiences do not have to be the same for everyone
- Acknowledges the inherent value of the mentee
- Affirms that the mentee is being listened to and understood and not being judged
- Builds trust and rapport in the mentoring relationship
- Reinforces a mentee's strengths and unique gifts

The Downside When The Validator Role Is Abdicated

When a mentee does not feel accepted and understood by their mentor, they can feel rejected, ignored, judged, and even worthless.

Key Validator Skills

- Focus on the relationship, not the issue
- Find your mentee's validation language
- Praise and validate effort
- Listen to the listening
- Recognize "validate" doesn't mean "agreeing with"

The Validator role provides an often-needed counterbalance to The Challenger. As The Validator, you communicate judgment-free acceptance and understanding of your mentee's thoughts and feelings. This doesn't mean you always agree with them, but that you support your mentee personally and want to continue to strengthen the mentoring relationship.

We all benefit from sincere, well-timed validation, as two of our greatest human needs are to be heard and be seen.

To be heard.

To be seen.

Let that sink in for a minute.

Does your mentee feel heard by you? For that matter, does your spouse or partner? Children? Team members? The Validator makes those important relationship investments while increasing trust, respect, and even love.

Focus on the Relationship, Not the Issue

Validating others doesn't come naturally to everyone. Many of us were raised in families or educational or professional environments where we were never validated. Horrifyingly, the first time my father ever told me he was proud of me was when I was thirty-two as I was leaving his mother's funeral. To the extent this describes your upbringing as well, you may need to consciously remind yourself to authentically and genuinely validate your mentee, and sometimes that's done after a pause. A pause after they've shared something unrelatable. A pause after they've shared something unrealistic or even fantastical. A pause when emotions are high, or an insecurity is surfacing. Or finally, a pause when they've shared something they're proud of that you may or may not find as praiseworthy against your own benchmark of success, but even a small validation could embolden them to keep going. The power of the pause—often a two- to three-second moment of silence—can result in a heightened feeling of authenticity. Sometimes, it's awkward or can feel uncomfortable. But resultingly, what you say next has an elevated impact as it's intentionally separated from a knee-jerk or rote verbal response. It communicates investment and thoughtfulness. It's the difference between saying, "Oh that's cool . . ." or "Good for you . . ." and "I just listened carefully to what you said, and I'm really impressed at the logic you've employed to come to that conclusion. That's a skill—even a superpower you have—and I want to ensure that you hear me and own it."

The Validator can also choose to push pause on a monumental issue their mentee is facing and pivot to investing in and strengthening the relationship by reminding them of even small wins that when compounded become the formula for successful momentum. Such as, "I see a strength in you that is common in very successful people. And that is, they resist becoming overwhelmed by the enormity of their goal and instead, metaphorically put one step in front of the other—just like you've done this week. I know there's still a ways to go, but keep up your consistent effort. It *will* pay off."

If, as a mentor, you are uncomfortable with emotions—both your own and those of your mentee—this role will require work. Consider six levels of validation from the work of American psychologist and author Dr. Marsha M. Linehan (she recommends using the highest level of validation you can in any situation):

- *Level 1: Presence.* Be present through active listening and be intentional about eye contact and nonverbal communication.

- *Level 2: Reflection.* Summarize what you hear your mentee saying in your own words.
- *Level 3: Guessing at Thoughts and Feelings.* Share what thoughts and emotions you feel your mentee is thinking/feeling and then validate if that's right.
- *Level 4: Understanding History.* Discuss what's currently happening as it relates to previously challenging experiences.
- *Level 5: Normalize Behavior.* Point out how their reaction is normal for the situation and shared by many others.
- *Level 6: Radical Genuineness.* Meet your mentee as an equal and express support, believing they can solve their own issues.

Find Your Mentee's Validation Language

Some of you may know I am privileged to host what is now the world's largest weekly leadership podcast for FranklinCovey, *On Leadership with Scott Miller.* In this role, I moderate weekly interviews, on video and audio, with remarkable authors, thought leaders, business titans, actors, athletes, researchers, and celebrities. After nearly three hundred episodes, one of my favorites is Dr. Gary Chapman, the renowned psychologist and author of the insanely popular book *The 5 Love Languages.* Is there even anyone left in a romantic relationship that hasn't read or listened to this book?

The premise of Dr. Chapman's book is that after decades of providing therapy to couples, his notes and research showed one repeated theme with couples in serious conflict: Almost word for word, one of them would say, "Well, I just don't feel loved by [him/her] . . ."

As a result, Dr. Chapman identified what he calls the 5 Love Languages:

- Words of Affirmation
- Quality Time
- Acts of Service
- Gifts
- Physical Touch

I won't spend time here elaborating on them other than to say a key insight I've taken from the multiple times I've interviewed Dr. Chapman is to be aware that how we give love is often mirrored by how we wish to receive love (and that's not always a healthy congruence). We can apply this *principle* to The Validator, recognizing the clear boundaries that separate a romantic pursuit from a mentoring relationship. And in case you missed this point, let me say it again: In no way should you construe that *The 5 Love Languages* is your "to-do" list as a mentor. Validation does not mean love, as you can validate someone you don't like. The larger and salient point here is that, with emotions, we have individual preferences and comfort levels. Appropriately mirroring the *style* of your validation to one that aligns with what your mentee values will be affirming.

Said another way, we've all heard the Golden Rule as "Do unto others how you would have them do unto you." To which I say, "HOGWASH!"

The Validator is not focused on treating others how they *themselves* want to be treated. This is selfish and shortsighted. Instead, they practice what's known as the Platinum Rule: "Treat others how *they* want to be treated."

What's your mentee's validation language? If you've invested empathetic and focused time with them, you shouldn't have to guess. Nor should you have to ask something as awkward as "Now, before we get started, please tell me *exactly* how I should validate you through the mentoring process so I can make you feel heard and seen. Also, it would be helpful to know when you need a pick-me-up so I can be prepared in advance." As I reread that sentence, it feels like a line Sheldon Cooper would deliver on *The Big Bang Theory* sitcom (I fly a lot, so I've watched every episode . . . multiple times). Don't be tempted to go "Sheldon Cooper" with your mentee. Asking them for a point-by-point instruction manual for how you validate them shows you don't care enough to put in the time and effort to understand that for yourself.

Restating a key insight from my discussions with Dr. Chapman is to remind yourself that it's easy to provide others with the type of "love" in the same way you want to receive it. It's a trap many couples enter in romantic relationships. I like gifts, so I give gifts. I want to be affirmed verbally, so I affirm verbally. It's important not to confuse your love language (validation language) with that of your mentee. Pay the price to understand what will make them feel genuinely validated, and the result will be invaluable: increased trust and momentum toward them accomplishing their goals.

Praise and Validate Effort

If your mentee seems significantly limited by their entrenched mindsets, remember such feelings can be inculcated in us early in life by our parents, caregivers, extended family, educators, clergy, and people we see as authority figures. The Validator not only looks to support and affirm their mentee when they're feeling confused, frustrated, or stalled, but also when they have a win, a break-through, or are gaining momentum toward their goal. You may or may not see their achievement or milestone as significantly as they do, but as The Validator, you can praise effort and growth, so the mentee knows they're on the right track. But do this judiciously and sincerely—it's easy to feel patronized if you're on the receiving end of overly proffered and undeserved praise.

Listen to the Listening

In another podcast interview, I featured British communication expert Julian Treasure, who authored the book *How to Be Heard*. His TED Talks have been viewed hundreds of millions of times where he promotes the adage "Listen to the listening." OK, forgive him for the awkward phraseology (being British, "American" is clearly his second language), but what he's saying is brilliant.

Listen to how the other person listens and communicate accordingly.

The Validator recognizes that how their mentee listens may not be how they, themselves, listen. And this matters because how we communicate is based on how we listen.

Take me, for example: I am loud. Like, really loud. I project like a megaphone without being burdened with actually holding one. Perhaps this is from suffering some hearing loss, so I don't calibrate my voice well or maybe deep down I have some psychological issue that results in the need to pummel others into submission by yelling/ bawling/shouting/screaming/wailing. (On second thought, let's go with the hearing-loss thing.) My point is, in the speeches I deliver, some portion of the audience loves me and is fully checked in *because* of my energy and volume, while some other large percentage is repelled by my vocal dynamics and my credibility plummets. This latter group finds my voice level fatiguing, which is why I hired a coach to train me to modulate my tone, rate, and pitch, hoping to meet everyone (or at least most) where they're at.

The Validator listens to the listening styles of other people and adjusts accordingly. So, if you and I ever meet, feel free to yell in my face.

Recognize "Validate" Doesn't Mean "Agreeing With"

An essential mindset of The Validator is recognizing that they can accept their mentee's thoughts and feelings while not agreeing with them. Validating your mentee's viewpoint builds trust and strengthens the relationship, even if you follow up with The Challenger (role #5) to call into question the viewpoint's veracity. You can see how The Validator, The Questioner (role #4), and The Challenger (role #5) often work hand in hand, affirming, clarifying, validating, and sometimes even challenging a mentee's mindset and behaviors. There is a vital interplay between the supportive, directive, and discovery goals of each, but without the trust that comes from The Validator's investment in the relationship, asking the mentee to think or act differently will probably fall short. Your intent is to make them feel heard and seen.

Here are some phrases you might draw from when you feel your mentee could benefit from being validated:

- I'd like to stop for a moment and call out something I see you doing/saying that I think is worthy of recognition.

- I see some clear progress/maturity/growth you've shown on this topic. Let's pause for a moment so you can own it. Truly, relish in it. I'm proud of you. I'm also learning from you.
- Stop. Did you see/hear/notice that? Do you notice the new direction you're taking? How is that feeling to you? Are you proud? I am.
- What an interesting way to think about this. I would never have thought to view/position/approach it in that way. I'm impressed with your creativity/ingenuity.
- You are amazingly resourceful/resilient/determined. These are skills that will become your brand and serve you well in life. Keep it up!
- I am impressed by how you . . .
- I truly enjoy meeting with you, and I'd like to tell you why. When we meet I, . . .

You can see from this list that there are many opportunities to deploy The Validator role. It doesn't have to be just within the context of a formal mentoring session; you could also simply pull your mentee aside and catch them in a moment that would feel praiseworthy to them. It could even be via email, text, or social media if appropriate.

The Validator Role and Me

Validation.

Seriously, who's suffering from too much validation in life? Not me. Thanks for that, Dad. I certainly was not overvalidated by my parents. In my home, it was guilty until proven innocent. And even then, I remained a person of interest. We hear these myths of a generation being coddled by an early life of participation ribbons, highlighted by Pittsburgh Steelers linebacker James Harrison who lamented about his sons' participation trophies on social media and then returned them. The truth is, as *USA Today* writer Charles LeClaire points out, "Something that feels like a participation trophy to Harrison might be perceived as hard-earned by others." That's an insight The Validator knows well.

I have a few, but impactful stories in my own life where someone (even accidentally) did, in fact, validate me. Even decades later, I can share, word for word, what they said. I can even tell you where I was standing or seated, what I was wearing or eating. The impact was so profound, I carried their words in a metaphorical backpack for when I needed to draw on them consciously or unconsciously during times of lean confidence.

Do not underestimate the lasting power of carefully chosen, well-spoken, and thoughtfully delivered validation. I only wish my father was alive to read this chapter—perhaps a bit too thin on the validation, Pop!

Captures—Additional Tools

PRE-MENTORING REFLECTION

Consider those who have played The Validator role in your life (this might include formal mentors, colleagues, parents, friends, teachers, and ecclesiastical leaders). Review which of the Key Validator Skills illustrated in the chapter opening that they demonstrated and describe the impact in your life:

_____

_____

_____

_____

_____

Capture the "big ideas" you have about The Validator role. Consider your own mentoring experiences. What in life has prepared you for this role? What might you need to do to prepare more? What can you adopt from the previous exercise? Write your thoughts below:

_____

_____

_____

_____

_____

IN-THE-MOMENT MENTORING PROMPTS

Revisit the questions and key insights found throughout The Validator chapter. These could include both questions for the mentee or reflection questions to help you with your mentoring mindset. Choose those that feel the most relevant given an upcoming mentoring session and write them below. If the questions are reflective in nature, take a moment to answer them for yourself.

Mentee Questions

Question 1:

_____

Question 2:

_____

Question 3:

_____

Question 4:

_____

Mentor Reflection Questions

Question 1:

_____

Answer:

_____

Question 2:

_____

Answer:

_____

Question 3:

_____

Answer:

_____

Question 4:

_____

Answer:

_____

Role 6: The Validator

POST-MENTORING LEARNING

Following your mentoring session, think back to how things went when adopting The Validator role. Some roles may feel more natural to you than others, but they all benefit from objectively assessing what worked, what didn't, and what you can learn as a result.

1. *Circle the answer that best corresponds to this statement:* "The Validator role was effective for me as a mentor during the mentoring session."

    a. Strongly agree
    b. Agree
    c. Neutral
    d. Disagree
    e. Strongly disagree

2. *Circle the answer that best corresponds to this statement:* "In the mentoring session, I achieved the Validator goal: 'To strengthen the mentoring relationship and progress their journey by strategically validating a mentee's confidence, competence, fears, and anxieties.'"

    a. Strongly agree
    b. Agree
    c. Neutral
    d. Disagree
    e. Strongly disagree

3. **Explore the "why" behind your answers.** Consider what
    worked and didn't in your mentoring session. What should
    you stop or start doing? What might you do less or more of?
    If you found gaps in your ability to execute this role, what can
    you do to close them? Capture your learning from this
    session and anything that, on reflection, could help you grow
    to be more comfortable and capable in this role:

    _____

    _____

    _____

    _____

Role 7: The Navigator

The Navigator leverages their knowledge and expertise to chart a way forward for their mentees. Whether having walked the path themselves or gained wisdom from the journey of others, they stay at least "a day ahead." The Navigator maps out the relevant opportunities, costs, best practices, regulations, processes, guidelines, and even laws that define, restrict, or serve as guideposts along the way.

The Goal

To draw on the mentor's wisdom and experience to guide the mentee away from potential pitfalls and toward their intended destination (also sometimes known as protecting people from themselves).

The Upside When The Navigator Role Is Employed Well

- Provides an opportunity to share the various insights gained by a mentor over their career
- Helps mitigate against career pitfalls and offer shortcuts along the mentee's journey
- Connects decision-making to governing principles
- Surfaces best practices
- Serves as a buffer against "unconscious incompetence"
- Provides focus and necessary guardrails to keep things on track and build momentum

The Downside When The Navigator Role Is Abdicated

The mentee can become a "wanderer," tempted to identify too many goals and quickly lose their focus on their unique path—one where the mentor's own life experience, institutional and industry knowledge, and hindsight could have proven valuable.

Key Navigator Skills

- Stay a day ahead
- Connect to governing principles
- Understand the situational rules of the road
- Minimize unconscious incompetence
- Keep perspective

The Navigator role reminds me of something annoying that my mother used to say: "I've been where you're going." I was too young, arrogant, and immature to give it any credence. Her point was to listen to her advice despite being from a different generation because there is hard-won wisdom that comes from having traveled the path before. As it turned out, her experiences were more relatable and valuable than I had thought. As a mentor, your experiences can provide the practical knowledge to keep your mentee from having to re-create the wheel. Your "been there, done that" wisdom is a massive gift you can offer (sparingly). I know what you're thinking: "Wait, this is contrary to everything this author has been talking about up until this point!" And you'd be right. But I learned a valuable lesson from my speech coach, Judy Henrichs, whom I referenced in The Boundary Setter (role #2), which is the art of knowing when to break established rules. As you enter the role of The Navigator, be aware that I'm going to soften the rules a bit around how much of your journey you should be sharing with your mentee. If they didn't want your experience, they would have had a peer mentor them. I intentionally overemphasized, early on in this book, the cautions around sharing your experiences and journeys so that you would be hypersensitive to how easy it is to fall into that self-referenced narrative. My sense is now you're sufficiently heightened in your awareness and will proceed as is appropriate.

Stay a Day Ahead

I recently had a conversation with middle school educator and TikTok superstar Gabe Dannenbring. He's a talented, passionate, and gifted educator currently tasked with teaching science to seventh graders—something that isn't his real expertise. (Gabe earns five times an educator's salary as a social media influencer but simply loves teaching and mentoring students.) When I asked him about teaching a subject not necessarily his passion or even expertise, his response was, "I only need to be one day ahead of the students to make it work well." Gabe is a dynamic guy, and you can tell instantly from meeting him how quickly he can capture his students' attention and respect. But he recognizes he can play the role of The Navigator, even in a content area that isn't his personal passion or educational expertise, and still inspire and teach his students.

What "one day ahead" means inside a classroom of teenagers is different in a mentoring context. "One day ahead" is not a literal descriptor for what the mentor should know ahead of time. Rather, it is a principle that simply means *be informed enough about your mentee's journey that you, even if you haven't traveled the entire path yourself, can still call out what's likely ahead.* Perhaps you began your career as a serial entrepreneur while your mentee has their sights on a straight-lined trajectory inside a single organization. Or you're a twenty-year veteran of a single department and your mentee needs to strategically bounce from division to division to gain the experiences and knowledge to deploy later in life. Such potential for mentor-mentee career congruence or detachment will manifest in the seemingly endless number of possibilities and circumstances surrounding your mentees' goals. Be prepared to be agile in your thinking so you can articulate the next likely or logical steps that will keep them moving in the right direction. Disclaimer: I recognize this previous paragraph is ambitious for all mentors and is easier said (written) than done. So don't be too overwhelmed. Rather, be well-read, well-practiced, and a lifelong learner.

Connect to Governing Principles

There are proven processes and principles that most of us follow in life. Dr. Stephen R. Covey called them governing principles because they are timeless, apply to everyone, and cross every culture, generation, and industry. Such governing principles don't change—they are everlasting with predictable outcomes for following or violating them. The Navigator can help connect decisions, via governing principles, to predicable outcomes, like this:

- Making and keeping commitments versus avoiding and breaking them will define your reputation and brand, for good or bad.
- Building and maintaining mutually beneficial relationships versus using others as a means to an end will manifest as a competitive advantage or create a culture of disdain and quiet (and not so quiet) quitting.
- Offering excuse-laden versus excuse-free apologies will either engender trust or breed resentment and skepticism (for more on professional relationship building, read Todd Davis's bestseller *Get Better: 15 Proven Practices to Build Effective Relationships at Work*).

Part of The Navigator's role is connecting present *cause* to future *effect*. Projecting where a course of action will take your mentee based on governing principles can save them the pain of an unwanted outcome or sometimes even provide a shortcut to greater benefits. So when in The Navigator role, don't hesitate to remind your mentee of the natural consequences of pursuing the path in debate. Principles are ever-present and for every action there is a reaction. Sometimes positive, sometimes negative. The Navigator helps bring those principles and consequences to life. Not in a threatening or punitive way, but in a pragmatic and wise way. In short, you're Yoda helping a young Padawan more effectively reach their goals.

Understand the Situational Rules of the Road

Simply stated, The Navigator creates a "how to" map—how to open a particular business, get promoted within this organization, spin out and increase their income, start a side hustle, earn a law degree, etc. This doesn't mean as The Navigator that you're going to be an expert in everything. Of course, you can't be. To quote author and leadership expert Wanda T. Wallace, who wrote the book *You Can't Know It All,* your mentee won't expect you to "know it all" and nor should you expect that from yourself. However, you should be both building and drawing upon a broad base of knowledge, including having a working understanding of perhaps some of the items below:

- Financial and accounting processes
- Reading a P&L
- Calculating margin and EBITDA
- Understanding profit margins and cash flow
- Determining a business's money-making model

- Identifying what author and consultant Ram Charan calls the "5 Parts of Business: Cash, Margin, Velocity, Customers, and Growth"
- Health standards and other legal requirements as applicable
- An understanding of potential career paths
- Overall organizational structure of the employing organization and how roles might build on each other
- Knowledge of the divisions of growth and which leaders might be best to develop their skills
- Their own brand and reputation (what kind of reputation have they "behaved themselves into")
- What skills, talents, and competencies they need to develop to stay relevant in a changing marketplace
- What skills they need to refine to ensure their own career development with their current employer
- Managing and resolving conflict with others
- Key personality, communication, and listening traits that can work for or against them
- Their interpersonal skills—do they seek or avoid conflict with others?
- Their self-awareness and ability to self-regulate
- Goal-setting methodology and execution strategies
- Building focus and discipline
- What tools to employ to keep them focused on their goals and priorities in a world barraged by distractions
- Understanding natural consequences
- Connecting decisions to outcomes
- Decision gates and contingency planning

- High-value decision-making
- Differentiating between what's urgent and important
- Separating strategy from tactics

Horrified?

Don't be. This list is quite intimidating to some prospective mentors because there's a seemingly endless number of areas you might feel the need to be competent in. It's not reasonable. But what does seem reasonable is that as The Navigator, you can be "one day" ahead of your mentee and that may be as simple as being the person holding the flashlight on any of the above. As you help uncover and identify your mentee's goals, that may necessitate you engaging in some research or learning on a particular topic to ensure your relevance and value-add. Remember, depending on your mentee's goals, being "one day ahead" can mean different things.

Minimize Unconscious Incompetence

You could think of each of the previously mentioned bullets as crossroads a mentee will face. This is why combining the roles of The Navigator and The Questioner (role #4) can be valuable in early brainstorming conversations. Such unconscious incompetence, also known as *not knowing what we don't know,* can be a career, if not life-limiting, deficit. The Navigator can help minimize this some. And isn't that what life is mostly about? Minimizing our mistakes through knowledge so we can unleash our unique talents and passions to achieve what matters most? Rachel Hollis, the famed author and social influencer, said to me once in a podcast interview: "Knowledge is power. When applied correctly." And Jill Koziol,

CEO and co-founder of Motherly, said, "The role of an entrepreneur is not to take as many risks as possible—it's to mitigate as many of them as possible."

This may also be a great opportunity to demonstrate your own growth from incompetence to competence or from a limiting belief to one that's empowering. As The Navigator, you're encouraged to share as many of your own relevant and relatable experiences in the hopes your mentee, with perhaps some courage, chooses to move outside of their comfort zones. Think of times in your life when you learned something new through an unfamiliar or uncomfortable experience. Maybe it was your first foreign trip, a friendship or romantic relationship with someone from outside your normal cultural upbringing, a college subject you took and excelled in despite your high school experience. Or maybe it was even a work assignment that required you to learn new skills and stretch your self-confidence against a crippling sense of self-doubt. We've all been unconsciously (or even consciously) incompetent at some point or another. And while I don't suggest you use those exact words in your mentoring (at least not in the first thirty minutes), you can certainly share your journey as part of The Navigator role.

Keep Perspective

Independent of a trauma or serious personal violation, try to help your mentee keep perspective. When viewed in the larger context of life and what they're going to face, look for opportunities to turn any setbacks into learnings. The Navigator makes use of not only their journey but what they've learned about their mentee as well, likely as The Absorber (role #3) and The Questioner (role #4).

Maybe Charles Swindoll's adage "Life is 10 percent what happens to you and 90 percent how you react to it" might be helpful. I've also come to love the phrase "Sometimes a disappointment turns into an appointment." Maybe you can explore with your mentee what that appointment looks like through a healthy, rational, and logical perspective.

The Navigator Role and Me

I intentionally listed several entrepreneur and solopreneur concerns in this chapter, as nowadays everyone seems to have a side hustle. The creator economy is alive and well. Globally, it has empowered people to build their own business and control their own future.

Exciting.

Invigorating.

Daunting.

Loosely quoted by American author and radio host Dave Ramsey, one of our generation's experts on personal finance: "A paycheck is what an organization offers you to give up on your own dreams."

That sure haunted me, especially after thirty years of receiving a paycheck from employers. Only now in my fifties have I become an entrepreneur. I can't help but wonder, *Did I give up on my dreams for too long?* Be sure to see the other side of Dave's advice and recognize that not everyone wants or should be an entrepreneur. I have little to no regrets about how I built my career and what I learned while "taking a paycheck" (because for me "taking a paycheck" meant busting my ass). I am now deftly employing those learnings in my many books, podcasts, courses, coaching, and keynotes. I never would have had the level of success I am experiencing now without those three decades having gladly accepted those paychecks.

I also co-own a literary, speaking, and talent agency called Gray + Miller (graymilleragency.com). We represent hundreds of expert speakers; help produce movies, documentaries, and television content; and represent agents and their authors to sell their book manuscripts to publishers. One author we represent is Melinda Emerson, known as the Small Biz Lady, and author of *Become Your Own Boss in 12 Months*. This book is a practical how-to guide (literally a step-by-step road map for entrepreneurs to read and follow) BEFORE THEY QUIT THEIR DAY JOB AND FOLLOW THEIR DREAMS OF OWNING A BUSINESS.

The book is superb, but I have to acknowledge that when I first started reading it, I found it somewhat elementary (mainly because I was arrogant and unconsciously incompetent). But I quickly came to appreciate the intentional simplicity of Melinda's advice and how practical and vital her recommendations were for someone like me, pivoting from a three-decade career ensconced in a large company with vast resources—people and financial—to preparing to go solo as an entrepreneur. What Melinda provides is a step-by-step navigation for how to better ensure your success as an entrepreneur. I feel like her book is the perfect manifestation of what The Navigator role can do with a mentee, regardless of what their goal is. And while I benefited tremendously from her book, I can't help but wonder, had I additionally had a Navigator mentor, how many pitfalls might I have avoided, and what shortcuts might I have found? We all can benefit from the wisdom of a mentor playing The Navigator role in our lives.

Don't shortchange the breadth and depth of your experience, regardless of the road you traveled to get there. You have a mentee who will benefit from it, if you're willing to share it sparingly and wisely and help them chart their way forward.

Captures—Additional Tools

PRE-MENTORING REFLECTION

Consider those who have played The Navigator role in your life (this might include formal mentors, colleagues, parents, friends, teachers, and ecclesiastical leaders). Review which of the Key Navigator Skills illustrated in the chapter opening that they demonstrated and describe the impact in your life:

_____

_____

_____

_____

_____

Role 7: The Navigator

Capture the "big ideas" you have about The Navigator role. Consider your own mentoring experiences. What in life has prepared you for this role? What might you need to do to prepare more? What can you adopt from the previous exercise? Write your thoughts below:

_____

_____

_____

_____

_____

IN-THE-MOMENT MENTORING PROMPTS

Revisit the questions and key insights found throughout The Navigator chapter. These could include both questions for the mentee or reflection questions to help you with your mentoring mindset. Choose which feel the most relevant to an upcoming mentoring session and write them below. If the questions are reflective in nature, take a moment to answer them for yourself.

Mentee Questions

Question 1:

_____

Question 2:

_____

Question 3:

_____

Question 4:

_____

Mentor Reflection Questions

Question 1:

_____

Answer:

_____

Question 2:

_____

Answer:

_____

Question 3:

_____

Answer:

_____

Question 4:

_____

Answer:

_____

POST-MENTORING LEARNING

Following your mentoring session, think back to how things went when adopting The Navigator role. Some roles may feel more natural to you than others, but they all benefit from objectively assessing what worked, what didn't, and what you can learn as a result.

1. *Circle the answer that best corresponds to this statement:* "The Navigator role was effective for me as a mentor during the mentoring session."

   a. Strongly agree

   b. Agree

   c. Neutral

   d. Disagree

   e. Strongly disagree

2. *Circle the answer that best corresponds to this statement:* "In the mentoring session, I achieved the Navigator goal: 'To draw on the mentor's wisdom and experience to guide the mentee away from potential pitfalls and toward their intended destination (also sometimes known as protecting people from themselves).'"

   a. Strongly agree

   b. Agree

   c. Neutral

   d. Disagree

   e. Strongly disagree

3. **Explore the "why" behind your answers.** Consider what worked and didn't in your mentoring session. What should you stop or start doing? What might you do less or more of? If you found gaps in your ability to execute this role, what can you do to close them? Capture your learning from this session and anything that, on reflection, could help you grow to be more comfortable and capable in this role:

_____

_____

_____

_____

_____

Role 8:
The Visionary

The Visionary paints a picture of the future to inspire their mentee to take on new challenges, see themselves as more capable, or envision an expanded outcome. The Visionary artfully tempers such a vision, however, so it remains motivating and achievable, not so grandiose as to be unactionable, or reflective of what the mentor values and not the mentee.

The Goal

To provide a vision of a future state that stretches the mentee to do and become more, yet remain grounded within their motivations and present (or reasonably acquirable) skills.

The Upside When The Visionary Role Is Employed Well

- Creates a motivating picture of what the mentee can achieve
- Anchors day-to-day work to something bigger
- Helps a mentee reach their full potential
- Sets the stage for moving the conceptual into concrete actions

The Downside When The Visionary Role Is Abdicated

Decouples a mentee's day-to-day work from a vision of what they're working toward, making it less likely they'll offer discretionary effort or make any real progress toward their articulated goals.

Key Visionary Skills

- Speak your future truth
- Be thoughtful about what's realistically possible
- Find a new summit instead of new mountains
- Ensure it's the mentee's vision and not yours
- Calibrate your conversation

The word *visionary* is often attached to some of the most effective and charismatic leaders we talk about. They are the leader we want to follow and the mentor we want to learn from. With names like Disney, Winfrey, Gates, Jobs, and Blakely, visionaries often cast a long shadow. They are the big-picture thinkers who see no obstacle as too difficult to overcome and no future as too unobtainable to strive toward. And sometimes they're perfectionists, control freaks, egomaniacs, micromanagers, and prolific dreamers who couldn't execute to save their lives. (I may have described many of your current and former leaders—or you, if you're self-aware enough to admit it.)

Welcome to the complexity of being The Visionary.

The Visionary role, however, is not about you stepping into some mythologized legacy. It's one of the thirteen roles identified in this book to be used situationally and appropriately as simply one tool in your mentoring tool belt. Yet it remains aspirational—The Visionary inspires a mentee to see themselves as a little more capable, their future a little bigger, and their trajectory a little less scripted than they might otherwise believe.

Speak Your Future Truth

As I've mentioned, I have the privilege of hosting two podcasts: one titled *C-suite Conversations with Scott Miller* and the other titled *On Leadership with Scott Miller*. (Note to budding radio, podcast, and television hosts, always put your name in the title. It's a proven principle that's lasted generations, beginning with *The CBS Evening News with Walter Cronkite*.) One of my favorite interviews was with the entrepreneur, YouTube sensation, and author Patrick Bet-David who wrote the bestseller *Your Next Five Moves*. (I highly recommended this book.) Of the many concepts Patrick teaches about strategic thinking, he shares a profound idea he calls "Your Future Truth." This roughly means identifying what you want to accomplish and then speaking as if it's true. This is a remarkably easy insight for The Visionary to share with their mentee. The logic goes like this: What you say impacts what you believe; what you believe impacts what you say. Together they impact how you behave.

Help your mentee see the congruency between how they think, what they say, how they behave, and the results that follow. Think about that in your own life! Consider reading *Your Next Five Moves* and teach your mentee (and yourself) how to turn a spoken future truth into a present reality.

Be Thoughtful about What's Realistically Possible

I'm notorious for telling (convincing) mentees and others that they can do anything. And it sometimes works out. But mostly it doesn't. I've come to learn my unbridled vision for people often excites them in the beginning, but ultimately, they can't live up to the vision I've painted for them. Here are some actual things I've said to mentees:

- "Of course, you can totally speak in front of three thousand people next week. Let's just role-play a few times. Watch this video of me doing it and you'll be just fine!"
- "Yes, you can develop an entirely new deck to show the board how we can deliver $2 million in profit by the end of the year. And don't forget about all those Excel pivot tables you'll need to build, but don't worry, you'll nail it!"
- "You want to give snow skiing a try? Absolutely, you can do it, and don't worry about having lived in Florida your

entire life. I'll take you to the mountains and you'll be crushing the black diamond runs by noon!"

These vision statements ended poorly. Some very poorly. One involving a stretcher pulled by the ski patrol.

When you notice something remarkable in your mentee and sense they're capable of seeing and setting new boundaries, this is your opening and I suggest you go for it! Just be mindful that The Visionary role can be invigorating. It can ignite latent creativity, unrealized genius, and expand someone's idea of what's possible. It can create a path stretching beyond their perceived reach. It can positively affect a mentee's self-esteem and self-confidence. But if you're not thoughtful about what's realistically possible for your mentee, it can have the opposite effect as well—crushing them into failure and cementing a mindset that associates not just risk but outright failure with venture. Be cautious that the person who is being invigorated isn't you but rather your mentee. Too often mentors play The Visionary role in the hopes of living vicariously through their mentee.

Find a New Summit Instead of New Mountains

The Visionary is thoughtful about finding new summits on an existing journey versus pointing out whole new mountains to climb. Not that the latter isn't possible or even warranted sometimes, but a more actionable picture for The Visionary to paint extends the trajectory the mentee is already on, perhaps higher and further, by leveraging their existing momentum. This is helpful because their journey thus far (which you've been involved with as you move through the thirteen roles of mentorship) provides data about what your mentee *is* doing today and what they *could* do tomorrow.

To help create such a vision, consider this:

- Stepping back from the "day-to-day" tasks often surfacing as the urgent priorities on your mentee's calendar. Setting a vision requires room to think and time in the "eye of the storm."
- Making sure the vision you're setting with your mentee is aligned to the values and objectives of their employing organization (if that's relevant).
- Inviting your mentee to reflect on both personal and professional outcomes, as they are often intertwined.
- Discussing your role after the vision's been set—how can you best support your mentee moving forward? (You can offer the thirteen roles in this book as a guide for them to choose from and determine which might be best for them to continue leveraging, from you or a future mentor.)
- Preparing your mentee for the resilience required to turn a vision into reality. If the thought of hard work dissuades them, it's likely the wrong vision.
- Inviting "visioning" brainstorming but keep it attached to reaching a new summit versus climbing a new mountain.
- Making sure the vision feels compelling enough to be motivating but practical enough that it doesn't feel unobtainable.
- Committing to communicate often to keep the vision relevant, tactical, and from drifting into the conceptual.

Ensure It's the Mentee's Vision and Not Yours

The Visionary resists outlining a grandiose vision for what *they* would and could do. Instead, they are hyperfocused on what their mentee's capabilities, aspirations, talents, drive, motivation, skills—and a host of other concerns that will surface through the mentoring process—infer. The Visionary checks themselves for any future goal attainment that feels like a slam dunk for them but would end up being a major (and even risky) stretch for the mentee.

Calibrate Your Conversation

Here are some conversations you might have to help calibrate your role as The Visionary:

- "I like your current thinking about this direction. How would you feel if we brainstormed together all the future possibilities and even expansions and then talked straight about what's possible and realistic to ensure you're set up for success?"
- "I want to be certain not to distract you from executing the path we've discussed and agreed to, so how about sometime soon, we discuss the risks and rewards of a broader, bigger vision?"
- "I've found a commonality in people who actually accomplish the professional goals they set for themselves: They navigate the precarious balance between a heads-down focus on the here and now with a bold vision for what could be in the future. Let's talk about how to

ensure you tack back and forth between those two so that you see the upside long term and win on both."

- "I have an idea . . . what if we took fifteen minutes and just brainstormed all the possibilities of expanding your current plan? Then you select what you think is the best idea and then agree on a step-by-step process of how to achieve it. After that, we could put in some milestones and release you to create the future you never thought possible."
- "The lead author of the best-selling book, *The 4 Disciplines of Execution*, Chris McChesney, says, 'There will always be more good ideas than there is capacity to execute.' This is applicable both with organizations and individuals. Let's be sure we're mindful of balancing your vision with your capacity to execute—with excellence."

There may be perfect circumstances when the benefit of your creativity and vision as a mentor is exactly what's needed. Perhaps someone is on the cusp of a massive pivot in their already successful career. Or their entrepreneurial business is at the tipping point of exploding (positively). Or conversely, their own successful company or solid side hustle is getting its arse kicked by more nimble competition and your mentee needs a major lifeline. Like they need you to pull out all the stops and offer them your finest vision of what could be (and what might save their bacon).

This may be your finest day as a mentor: the culmination of all your battles and wars cast into a vision of what's possible.

This is awesome.

This is satisfying.

This is also very rare.

The Visionary Role and Me

I am incapable of thinking small. I don't mean being a small thinker (socially or politically) but thinking small in terms of scale. I only think big. Like really, really big. Sometimes even irresponsibly big.

To quote my recently passed father, who never worried about my ability to support myself or my big thinking, "Scott has champagne taste on a beer budget."

True dat, Pops.

My father then went on to be a role model and teach me how to create a champagne budget through old-fashioned hard work, which has become, later in life, my hallmark (and we're teaching our three sons the same—you can have anything you want in life if you work hard enough for it.) This might seem naive for some, but I believe it to be directionally true.

As a result, I'll admit . . . I want a great home, a showplace actually. A really nice car, elegant custom-fit shirts, an amazing Italian vacation with my family, the biggest product launch, the most outrageous conference opening, and so on. Everything I do in life is to one-up—not you, but myself. I rarely, if ever, consciously compare myself to anyone else. Instead, I obsessively compare my current self to my former self. I don't have the explanation for why this is so—ask my therapist . . . when I find one.

Sure, I like to impress others. I'm human. But I think of myself as a visionary—and it's not always valuable. Come to my event and you'll be impressed. Take a ride in my car and you'll wish you had it (just not my monthly payment). Come to my dinner parties and you're likely to be impressed. (Tip: Serve lots of champagne and a great appetizer up front, then as your guests get a bit sloshed, your meal can suck because they won't remember it—as several of my meals have been burnt or tasteless.)

But get on a mentoring call with me and I can quickly overwhelm you with a drastically expanded vision of what you were thinking, resulting in your complete paralysis. Or, in some cases, my mentee sees my vision and matches it with one even greater. It can go either way. Here are some reactions mentees have had to me in this mode:

- Lighting up with excitement and recalibrating their plans by expanding their vision
- Becoming overwhelmed at what I'm suggesting and shutting down completely
- Beginning to blindly chase after the new vision until they fail because it wasn't *theirs* and/or it wasn't based on a realistic assessment of their skills, passions, and talents
- Or any other combination of intended or unintended consequences

Use great judgment about when your own visioning skills are right for the circumstance. You have the power to end the day après-ski in front of a great pot of cheese fondue and a glass of champagne or sitting together in the emergency clinic holding your mentee's hand as the surgeon sets their broken leg.

Captures—Additional Tools

PRE-MENTORING REFLECTION

Consider those who have played The Visionary role in your life (this might include formal mentors, colleagues, parents, friends, teachers, and ecclesiastical leaders). Review which of the Key Visionary Skills illustrated in the chapter opening that they demonstrated and describe the impact in your life:

_____

_____

_____

_____

Capture the "big ideas" you have about The Visionary role. Consider your own mentoring experiences. What in life has prepared you for this role? What might you need to do to prepare more? What can you adopt from the previous exercise? Write your thoughts below:

_____

_____

_____

_____

_____

IN-THE-MOMENT MENTORING PROMPTS

Revisit the questions and key insights found throughout The Visionary chapter. These could include both questions for the mentee or reflection questions to help you with your mentoring mindset. Choose which feel the most relevant to an upcoming mentoring session and write them below. If the questions are reflective in nature, take a moment to answer them for yourself.

Mentee Questions

Question 1:

_____

Question 2:

_____

Role 8: The Visionary

Question 3:

_____

Question 4:

_____

Mentor Reflection Questions

Question 1:

_____

Answer:

_____

Question 2:

_____

Answer:

_____

Question 3:

_____

Answer:

_____

Question 4:

_____

Answer:

_____

POST-MENTORING LEARNING

Following your mentoring session, think back to how things went when adopting The Visionary role. Some roles may feel more natural to you than others, but they all benefit from objectively assessing what worked, what didn't, and what you can learn as a result.

1. *Circle the answer that best corresponds to this statement:* "The Visionary role was effective for me as a mentor during the mentoring session."

   a. Strongly agree

   b. Agree

   c. Neutral

   d. Disagree

   e. Strongly disagree

2. *Circle the answer that best corresponds to this statement:* "In the mentoring session, I achieved the Visionary goal: 'To provide a vision of a future state that stretches the mentee to do and become more, yet remain grounded within their motivations and present (or reasonably acquirable) skills.'"

   a. Strongly agree

   b. Agree

   c. Neutral

   d. Disagree

   e. Strongly disagree

3. **Explore the "why" behind your answers.** Consider what worked and didn't in your mentoring session. What should you stop or start doing? What might you do less or more of? If you found gaps in your ability to execute this role, what can you do to close them? Capture your learning from this session and anything that, on reflection, could help you grow to be more comfortable and capable in this role:

    _____

    _____

    _____

    _____

    _____

Role 9:
The Flagger

The Flagger works like their namesake on a construction site, intervening as necessary, with highly directive signs ("Stop" and "Caution") to protect their mentees from potential dangers.

The Goal

To appropriately intervene when it's necessary to slow down or stop a mentee and provide clarity around the potential pitfalls ahead.

. . .

The Upside When The Flagger Role Is Employed Well

- Stops a mentee from going down a path that could be dangerous, illegal, risky, or otherwise unsafe given the lay of the land
- Slows a mentee down so the mentor can offer feedback and allow the mentee to course-correct accordingly
- Benefits from and helps build trust that the mentor is looking out for the mentee
- Prevents "accidents" before they happen
- Reinforces the parameters set by The Boundary Setter (role #2)

The Downside When The Flagger Role Is Abdicated

Allows the mentees' ignorance and even arrogance to land them in metaphorical potholes.

Key Flagger Skills

- Raise the red "Stop" sign
- Raise the yellow "Caution" sign
- Choose your words carefully
- Declare your intent

In traffic control, a "flagger" is someone who directs vehicle traffic around construction sites. They help motorists and workers avoid the dangers of the active site. Likewise, The Flagger role guides mentees through various "work sites" where the risk of running into an obstacle or an unobtainable vision could be high. Unlike The Navigator (role #7), who is focused on the future, or The Challenger (role #5), who is pressing on an assumption or belief, The Flagger is fully engaged in the *present* and poised to intervene for the mentee's benefit. Depending on the inherent risks in a project, team, or culture, the time a mentor may need to spend in The Flagger role can vary. But when it comes time to raise a metaphorical sign to stop, slow, or redirect a mentee, they're ready and able to do so.

You may think, *This isn't my role, her leader should tell her this, or his wife or their parent needs to take this on* . . . and many times, this may be true. But please don't use that as a reason to put your signs down and walk away. Remember, just because you're a leader, or a spouse, or a parent, you weren't automatically infused with wisdom and courage. But The Flagger role will require a good deal of both.

Raise the Red "Stop" Sign

The Flagger is equipped with two important signs: the red "Stop" sign and the yellow "Caution" sign. Of primary concern is the "Stop" sign. The Flagger raises it (metaphorically) to stop the mentee in their tracks and essentially announces, "OK, you need to pull over . . . right now. Park, turn the engine off, and grab your keys— we're going for a walk."

Enacting this level of intervention requires courage. And sometimes your mentee will need such from you, whether consciously or unconsciously, to pull them over and sober them up. This might sound like the following:

- "Tim, that's not a healthy or—if you're honest with yourself—even an accurate assessment of what you're really dealing with."
- "My sense from having mentored many early-stage entrepreneurs is that you've got great intuition. However, your inexperience and ignorance in this realm is dangerously close to crushing you."
- "All of us in life balance between confidence and arrogance and I need to tell you that you're leaning more one way than the other . . . can I tell you *why* I think that?"
- "If you do what you're saying, then I need you to fully understand the consequences."
- "If you proceed with that plan, let me tell you what the end game will look like—maybe not in the short run, but absolutely in the long run."
- "I hear what you just said, and that horrifies me."
- "I need to stop you. What you just said is not only flat-out wrong, but borderline unethical and illegal. Perhaps you're unaware of this and I'll always assume good intent with you, but I owe it to you to call this out and steer you in a better direction."

Like The Questioner (role #4), The Flagger clarifies in the face of ambiguity. But they do so because there is danger ahead, and so sometimes the appearance of a "Stop" sign can feel sudden and even harsh. But better that than an impending head-on collision.

Raise the Yellow "Caution" Sign

Sometimes The Flagger will want to slow a mentee down long enough to provide feedback and make a simple course correction. But the nature of the feedback doesn't warrant coming to a full stop, likely because the feedback is rather minor, or the culture around the project "work site" is fairly safe. The yellow "Caution" sign signals it's time to slow down and proceed with care. The mentee may decide to come to a full stop, check the way forward, and hit the gas, redirect their route, or proceed as planned, paying closer attention to the way ahead. Under the yellow "Caution" sign, how the mentor proceeds is their call. The Flagger simply slows the mentee down so they have the time and information necessary to move forward.

Whether raising the red "Stop" or yellow "Caution" sign, The Flagger is a truth teller, balancing a mentee's journey against the dangers on the road.

Choose Your Words Carefully

The Flagger exercises great discretion in their word choice so as not to turn off their mentee. Feedback is tough and none of us really want it. We know we need it, but I don't know anyone who wakes up in the morning and says, "Skip the coffee cake and latte—what I *really* want today is an ego enema. Yeah, that sounds awesome." Said another way, "Let me search out people with pent-up frustrations about me so I can invite their unfiltered opinions into my life." Instead, as The Flagger, try something like one of these approaches:

- "Peter, I'm going to interrupt you here because what you're expressing is, in fact, the exact opposite of what all my experience on this topic has taught me. Perhaps my mindset is outdated, but can I tell you what I'm thinking, and I'd really value your thoughtful response to it?"
- "Kara, I listened intently to your line of thinking and in the spirit of 'being in your boat rowing with you,' I need to call a time-out and challenge how you're defining success in this role because I simply don't agree."
- "Suzanne, you have proven to me you are a creative genius and, combined with your energy, a genuine force of nature. I love that in you. And (not *but*, rather *and*) I think at your current speed, which I also admire, you're glossing over some important steps that you would benefit from reconsidering. Let's take this time to pivot for a few minutes and outline each of them so you own whether you want to reconsider any of them."

Declare Your Intent

The Flagger can benefit by first declaring their intent given the potential abruptness of their message. It could sound like, "I'd like to offer some of what I've been thinking and I may not state it exactly right. I might use the wrong words and I may even ask for a do-over. My intent is to hold up a metaphorical stop sign and ask you to listen with the intent to understand my point and why I'm saying it. Then let's robustly discuss how we process it. I could be wrong, but my intuition is telling me you deserve to know exactly what I'm thinking."

Drawing on the adage "Absent facts, people make stuff up," it's vital that you express verbally what your intent is whenever the conversation might lend itself to confusion or even conflict. When you expressly state what your real intent is, it automatically lowers your mentee's reptilian brain response—which is to defend, deflect, explain, or even entrench themselves in their position. To quote Dr. Stephen R. Covey's eldest son, Stephen M. R. Covey, the author of the best-selling book, *The Speed of Trust*, "We judge ourselves by our intentions and others by their behavior." Declaring your intent allows you to practice one of Stephen M. R. Covey's *The 13 Behaviors of a High Trust Leader*: the ability to Talk Straight.

As a mentor, you may be that rare, even single person who's built the trust and rapport with your mentee to talk straight and tell them the truth. Or at least your truth about their journey. The same advice that applies to The Absorber (role #3) applies here: differentiate between your own opinions, emotions, and feelings and separate them from facts. As The Flagger, you know that laws and policies are not generally open to much interpretation. The Flagger is concerned with slowing things down enough, so the mentee knows *what* they are. Only then can the mentee decide if they want to follow or break them.

The Flagger Role and Me

When I was functioning as the chief marketing officer for FranklinCovey, I led a team of about thirty-five associates with five direct reports. One day after a meeting, one of them took me aside, closed the door (thankfully), and told me I owed a member of the team an apology.

I was horrified.

Defensive.

Indignant even.

But he didn't back down and I knew he was right. I'd said some things to a team member, whom I had high trust with and am still friends with nearly a decade later, but my remarks were insensitive and candidly diminishing in front of the larger team. Not my finest moment (or the last one either). It was sobering feedback from my direct report.

Another time, still in the role as CMO, I was approached by a more junior team member (who reported to someone a level down from me) who told me I had a ferocious personality. I thanked them, uncertain whether they intended it as a compliment or a criticism. I asked for some context and realized it was both. The more they shared with me how they defined *ferocious*, the more I sobered up to the fact that it was mostly a liability in their eyes—especially with relationships. Ferociously determined to get a week's worth of yard work done by noon on Saturday? Total asset. Ferociously pushing a team to artificially galvanize around a new corporate strategy? Less so. A lot less so.

My entire career has been three steps forward, one step back. Had it not been for mentors along the way playing the role of The Flagger, it would have looked more like three steps forward, four steps back. And we know where that would end up.

Captures—Additional Tools

PRE-MENTORING REFLECTION

Consider those who have played The Flagger role in your life (this might include formal mentors, colleagues, parents, friends, teachers, and ecclesiastical leaders). Review which of the Key Flagger Skills illustrated in the chapter opening that they demonstrated and describe the impact in your life:

Capture the "big ideas" you have about The Flagger role. Consider your own mentoring experiences. What in life has prepared you for this role? What might you need to do to prepare more? What can you adopt from the previous exercise? Write your thoughts below:

_____

_____

_____

_____

_____

IN-THE-MOMENT MENTORING PROMPTS

Revisit the questions and key insights found throughout The Flagger chapter. These could include both questions for the mentee or reflection questions to help you with your mentoring mindset. Choose which feel the most relevant to an upcoming mentoring session and write them below. If the questions are reflective in nature, take a moment to answer them for yourself.

Mentee Questions

Question 1:

_____

Question 2:

_____

Role 9: The Flagger

Question 3:
_____

Question 4:
_____

Mentor Reflection Questions

Question 1:
_____

Answer:
_____

Question 2:
_____

Answer:
_____

Question 3:
_____

Answer:
_____

Question 4:
_____

Answer:
_____

POST-MENTORING LEARNING

Following your mentoring session, think back to how things went when adopting The Flagger role. Some roles may feel more natural to you than others, but they all benefit from objectively assessing what worked, what didn't, and what you can learn as a result.

1. *Circle the answer that best corresponds to this statement:* "The Flagger role was effective for me as a mentor during the mentoring session."

   a. Strongly agree

   b. Agree

   c. Neutral

   d. Disagree

   e. Strongly disagree

2. *Circle the answer that best corresponds to this statement:* "In the mentoring session, I achieved the Flagger goal: 'To appropriately intervene when it's necessary to slow down or stop a mentee and provide clarity around the potential pitfalls ahead.'"

   a. Strongly agree

   b. Agree

   c. Neutral

   d. Disagree

   e. Strongly disagree

3. **Explore the "why" behind your answers.** Consider what worked and didn't in your mentoring session. What should you stop or start doing? What might you do less or more of? If you found gaps in your ability to execute this role, what can you do to close them? Capture your learning from this session and anything that, on reflection, could help you grow to be more comfortable and capable in this role:

_____

_____

_____

_____

_____

Role 10: The Distiller

U p until this point, it's my hope you found each of the first nine mentoring roles not only valuable, but situationally distinctive. As I mentioned in my opening, there will always be a little crossover when two or more roles feel similar, complementary, or even sometimes contradictory. My advice is, Don't fixate on that. Awareness of which role could be helpful in the moment is most of the value of this book. The coming two roles, The Distiller (role #10) and The Activator (role #11), have a lot of similarities. And they also have one clear differentiator: The Distiller role is focused on you and your mentee deciding together which strategies, projects, decisions, and so on warrant continued focus and execution. You're basically their brainstorming and distillation partner as you "brew" up something together. Whereby The Activator (role #11) is perhaps a little more powerful—even dangerously so—because you are holding your match up to their candle, signifying "Do this, not that." "Pursue this instead of that." "Elevate this, forget that." The difference between these two roles may be subtle and also profound—it's up to you which and when and how you choose to play either or both of them.

Additionally, as you will learn in this chapter, I've added a sub-role to The Distiller, called The Archivist. Not so much the court reporter, where everything is being captured, but rather a curator of ideas and actions worthy of future retrieval.

The Distiller/Archivist role artfully collects and prioritizes the insights and passions gained over the mentoring journey and processes the opportunities into a palatable and actionable offering for the mentee to choose to adopt (or not).

The Goal

To leverage the insights and learnings that come after a series of mentoring sessions, then refine and reduce the options into a focused opportunity for the mentee to consider.

The Upside When The Distiller Role Is Employed Well

- Combines the strengths of several roles and focuses them on a specific solution
- Filters through an overabundance of potential choices to help the mentee decide where to invest their time and energy

- Allows the mentor to apply an artful combination of roles, goals, and objectives for their mentees to digest and make their own

The Downside When The Distiller Role Is Abdicated

The mentee can feel lost and even paralyzed because of the plentitude of choices, options, and paths that have surfaced through previous mentoring sessions.

Key Distiller Skills

- Pull different "ingredients" together to create something new
- Bottle the mentoring experiences into a unique offering
- Filter out what's helpful and what's not
- Create and archive "recipes"

At the turn of the nineteenth century, American alcohol distillers were fiercely focused on improving their craft. Specifically, they wanted to develop a more efficient system for distillation, create a higher-quality product, produce it in greater quantity, and do so in less time. These are not dissimilar to The Distiller role in mentoring—they work to increase the efficiency and effectiveness of their mentoring sessions while realizing higher-quality outcomes.

Pull Different "Ingredients" Together to Create Something New

The Distiller artfully combines the other twelve roles, often working with them in tandem to focus the mentee on something new. Where other roles have likely surfaced important but "glacier-sized" ideas, The Distiller discerns, captures, and assembles them into something new and actionable. For example, they may draw on their investments made as The Absorber (role #3), combine the clarity surfaced by The Questioner (role #4) and The Challenger (role #5), the trust engendered by The Validator (role #6), and the spark produced by The Activator (role #11). Or they might tap into the future inspired by The Visionary (role #8), tempered by The Boundary Setter (role #2), and sped up by The Connector (role #12). The point is, The Distiller has had sufficient experience with their mentee, through most if not all thirteen roles, to offer specific solutions.

Bottle the Mentoring Experiences into a Unique Offering

As The Distiller, you want to be judicious with what falls through the sieve and into the bottle. In this role, it's about your collective sense of what should be pursued. Your goal is to aggregate and prioritize the ideas, discussions, and directions you both have deemed worthy of pursuing.

This might at first blush seem contrary to some of my initial advice in The Revealer (role #1). But where early in the relationship it was not your time to create your version of the *Pietà* (Michelangelo's masterpiece I mentioned in role #1), The Distiller takes the accumulative body of mentoring work and accepts the challenge, albeit with careful intentionality. As the mentor, you may help bottle the beverage, but ultimately, it's always up to the mentee whether it's appetizing and worth drinking (or not).

If you're getting the sense that I'm now giving you permission to do a lot of things I insisted you didn't in the beginning of this book, you are right. Arguably, The Distiller is where your experience, creativity, knowledge, insight, and expertise come together for the benefit of the mentee. It's likely that The Distiller is the most fun role to play as the mentor—like everything in life, it's all about timing. And now is the time.

Filter Out What's Helpful and What's Not

Mentoring can't all be about listening and asking strategic questions. At some point, your mentee wants your guidance. They need your wisdom and experience to help them determine which direction is best for them (after all, if they knew, they wouldn't need you). You should have a solid mentoring history and good rapport by the time you employ The Distiller role. As The Absorber (role #3), you've likely learned a lot about your mentee's interests and desires, and as The Questioner (role #4), you further refined that knowledge into more specific, actionable areas.

But which ideas, discussions, and directions are worth pursuing? Remember, together with your mentee, you're the sieve. What gets past your distillery gets bottled and sold. But this is where additional filtering can take a plethora of potential choices and reduce them to a clear and actionable outcome. Much of that is simply filtering out all the competing (and even worthwhile) ideas that have surfaced during your sessions, congealing them, and even hierarchically organizing them for the mentee to endorse themselves.

Create and Archive "Recipes"

The Distiller comes with a sub-role called The Archivist. In addition to co-creating and endorsing the mentee's future strategies, The Archivist is discreetly documenting worthy discussions for future retrieval, leverage, or even activation. In essence, The Distiller, when acting as The Archivist, records what's been distilled and keeps it for future reference as a kind of "recipe." They curate lessons learned, insights, and wisdom to ensure that the great ideas left on the cutting-room floor—especially the genius ones—aren't lost forever. As The Distiller/Archivist, you should consider collecting and building a sort of recipe book, replete with the commitments, takeaways, substitutions, and directions necessary for the mentee to succeed. Here are some categories you might be mindful of to record and archive:

- Significant changes and breakthroughs in mindsets
- Agreements to eliminate or minimize negative thoughts or self-defeating behaviors
- Commitments made to themselves and you
- Flashes of inspiration or genius that perhaps were "parked" because they were off topic but worth revisiting
- Worthy questions that went unanswered or were insufficiently answered for any number of reasons

- Moments of serious reflection that require the mentee to both learn something new or do something different in their behaviors
- Insights you as the mentor gained from watching your mentee grow and develop that you may want to adopt in your own life or with your family
- Special remembrances of your journey together that might be used as The Closer (role #13)

Combining The Distiller and The Archivist roles allows you, as the mentor, to creatively co-produce, co-prioritize, and even co-capture a blend of mentee "ingredients" both built on a shared history and also distilled into an actionable plan of current and future strategies.

Captures—Additional Tools

PRE-MENTORING REFLECTION

Consider those who have played The Distiller role in your life (this might include formal mentors, colleagues, parents, friends, teachers, and ecclesiastical leaders). Review which of the Key Distiller Skills illustrated in the chapter opening that they demonstrated and describe the impact in your life:

_____

_____

_____

_____

Capture the "big ideas" you have about The Distiller role. Consider your own mentoring experiences. What in life has prepared you for this role? What might you need to do to prepare more? What can you adopt from the previous exercise? Write your thoughts below:

_____

_____

_____

_____

_____

IN-THE-MOMENT MENTORING PROMPTS

Revisit the questions and key insights found throughout The Distiller chapter. These could include both questions for the mentee or reflection questions to help you with your mentoring mindset. Choose which feel the most relevant to an upcoming mentoring session and write them below. If the questions are reflective in nature, take a moment to answer them for yourself.

Mentee Questions

Question 1:

_____

Question 2:

_____

Question 3:

_____

Question 4:

_____

Mentor Reflection Questions

Question 1:

_____

Answer:

_____

Question 2:

_____

Answer:

_____

Question 3:

_____

Answer:

_____

Question 4:

_____

Answer:

_____

POST-MENTORING LEARNING

Following your mentoring session, think back to how things went when adopting The Distiller role. Some roles may feel more natural to you than others, but they all benefit from objectively assessing what worked, what didn't, and what you can learn as a result.

1. *Circle the answer that best corresponds to this statement:* "The Distiller role was effective for me as a mentor during the mentoring session."

   a. Strongly agree

   b. Agree

   c. Neutral

   d. Disagree

   e. Strongly disagree

2. *Circle the answer that best corresponds to this statement:* "In the mentoring session, I achieved the Distiller goal: 'To leverage the insights and learnings that come after a series of mentoring sessions, then refine and reduce the options into a focused opportunity for the mentee to consider.'"

   a. Strongly agree

   b. Agree

   c. Neutral

   d. Disagree

   e. Strongly disagree

3. **Explore the "why" behind your answers.** Consider what worked and didn't in your mentoring session. What should you stop or start doing? What might you do less or more of? If you found gaps in your ability to execute this role, what can you do to close them? Capture your learning from this session and anything that, on reflection, could help you grow to be more comfortable and capable in this role:

_____

_____

_____

_____

_____

Role 11:
The Activator

The Activator senses the right moment to light a spark that ignites their mentee's momentum, passions, or trajectory. The Activator is concerned with finding the right moment where their mentee would benefit from a carefully worded statement of encouragement and belief, fueling their drive to push harder, set even more ambitious goals, or stretch themselves in new and exciting ways.

The Goal

To ignite new levels of motivation and momentum at an intentionally impactful moment, reinforcing the mentor's faith in what their mentee can achieve.

The Upside When the Activator Role Is Employed Well

- Infuses newfound drive and motivation
- Helps close the gap between a mentee wanting to do something new and actually accomplishing it
- Shows the mentor's faith in their mentee and their capabilities

The Downside When the Activator Role Is Abdicated

Misses the crucial moment when a mentee is poised to take on something more but lacks the simple spark to see it come to life.

Key Activator Skills

- Know which message to ignite
- Look for the signals to "strike the match"
- Use your power carefully
- Create the spark, not the candle

The Activator provides the spark, offered at the right time, that ignites your mentee's passions. If we divide the behavioral world into motivation and ability camps, The Activator is squarely concerned with the former. Where The Validator (role #6) is investing in building the relationship and affirming a mentee's thoughts and beliefs, The Activator uses their words to ignite passion and drive in their mentees. They create momentum like a flywheel, a term Jim Collins coined in his seminal bestseller, *Good to Great*.

Know Which Message to Ignite

I've shared several key messages throughout this book. (Most marketers will now tell you it's necessary to repeat a message seven times before a consumer pays attention and is motivated to act.)

Buy a copy of this book for everyone you know.

Buy a *copy* of this book for everyone you know.

Buy a copy of *this* book for everyone you know.

Buy a copy of this *book* for everyone you know.

Buy a copy of this book *for* everyone you know.

Buy a copy of this book for *everyone* you know.

Buy a copy of this book for everyone *you* know.

Buy a copy of this book for everyone you *know*.

And yes, I upped it to "eight" as the onslaught of competing messages will only get worse, not better.

Knowing which message to ignite is a crucial mentor responsibility. It may seem counterintuitive, but in The Activator role, you *can* spark too many fires. As the mentor, you need to be careful you don't fall victim to your mentee's perhaps contagious passion, seemingly endless stream of brilliant ideas, or even infectious personality where you end up igniting every idea they offer . . . or you offer. Candidly, that's irresponsible. This role needs to be employed judiciously and will require you to determine which ideas, projects, strategies, or products you pour gas on and ignite.

In comedy, timing is everything. I learned this the hard way when I was in Brazil delivering a keynote speech. Although my Spanish is strong(ish), my Portuguese is nonexistent. Try giving a three-hour keynote where humor is one of your major assets and your translator repeats everything you say, twenty seconds later, and groups seven sentences together. The result was losing my punchlines for three hours! I wanted to die.

The Activator must understand timing—just as you can't punch up every line with a joke, a mentor can't activate every creative idea their mentee talks about. Remember to be careful to not only ignite those ideas that *you're* excited about but also watch carefully for the excitement in your mentee. When and how you activate specific ideas and goals is more important than you may realize. Sometimes holding your "gunpowder" for the right shot can have a disproportionately valuable impact on focusing your mentee.

Some people fall into a category called external processors where they say out loud everything they think. This is their way of discerning if they believe everything they're saying or are passionate about something they're saying, or aren't. They need to hear themselves say everything in order to make a judgment call on it. There's nothing wrong with this communication style, however, you, as the mentor, need to be aware if this is the communication circumstance you and they are in so you're not validating and igniting everything coming out of their mouths.

Look for the Signals to "Strike the Match"

Here are some signals to look for when employing The Activator, match in hand:

- Watch your mentee's body language. Even when you're meeting virtually, if you pay attention, you can tell when someone's energy and passion change by topic.
- Look for a repeat of ideas and areas of interest that keep resurfacing. There's a reason this is happening. That doesn't always mean a mentor should progress it, but pay attention. (If someone had activated every idea I was passionate about, I'd have 300 businesses by now with 295 of them in bankruptcy.)
- Ask your mentee:

  - What excites you?
  - What brings you joy and purpose? (Those are heavy words that we throw around perhaps a bit too loosely, so be deliberate when you ask them and be sure you're checked in during their response.)

- Describe when you were the happiest. What were you doing? Who were you with? What about these situations brought you into a state of happiness?
- Conversely, what sucks the life from you? What do you dread? When you want to hide or avoid something or someone, what's going on?

You never know when some of the most innocuous questions might stick with your mentee long after your call or meeting. Even long after your mentoring engagement.

Use Your Power Carefully

Don't underestimate your power as a mentor: positional power, utility power, principle-centered power, and for The Activator role, the power of your words. In most, if not all, mentor-mentee relationships, the mentor will be in some sort of position of power, and you should not take that lightly or ever abuse it. Anything you get excited about, the mentee may mirror that excitement. Anything you throw cold water on may also get abandoned or neglected. Use your power carefully and don't forget the consequential impact of your words and energy to activate exactly what's right. Not for you, but for your mentee.

Create the Spark, Not the Candle

The Activator role is not the equivalent of the mortgage banker who approves or denies a loan. You are not the green-lighter of their passions and projects. Your mentee needs to decide when and what to pursue, as this is their decision, not yours. However, recognize the well-timed, life-changing trajectory your endorsement might ignite. This is what I term *creating the spark, not the candle,* and this is specific to The Activator role. After all, you have plenty of input into your mentee's future via The Absorber (role #3), The Navigator (role #7), and The Visionary (role #8). But The Activator recognizes that sometimes their best intervention is simply to ignite the mix of passions, interests, goals, desires, or other motivating elements present in the mentee. A candle lights the way, but the spark lights the candle first.

The Activator Role and Me

When my first book released, it was a huge milestone in my journey to pivot from behind the scenes as a producer and director to the front-and-center role of the lead actor (or what's known somewhat arrogantly as being "the talent"). News flash . . . everyone in the production is "the talent." I'd spent twenty-seven years working behind the scenes, selling, promoting, marketing, and setting the stage for others. Candidly, I'd made many people wealthy and famous because of my sales and marketing talents.

Then there was a pivot in my confidence. I was serving as the CMO and executive vice president of business development for FranklinCovey, the world's largest and most trusted leadership development company. I was sitting in my office meeting with a consultant I'd hired to help me think through a new book we were considering writing. Not me as the author, but several other very competent people in the firm. Remember, I was backstage, and the backstage crew doesn't go on stage—not even after the curtain call to bow. They stay hidden where "they belong." Insulting, if you ask me, but sometimes they simply don't want the limelight (and maybe sometimes they do!). It's worth asking, I think. In Hollywood, sometimes actors become producers, but name me a producer who became an actor. It's very rare.

So, I'm brainstorming the many ways the identified authors might structure the book, including the tone, voice, types of stories, and even the physical layout of the book. I'd done this countless times in my career and it was natural for me to think up an architecture and then pitch it to the future authors for them to capitalize on and bring to life in *their* book. After a typical thirty minutes of me pacing around my office spouting a constant stream of ideas and prototypes, Leigh Stevens, a consultant, and friend, played The Activator role and looked at me with complete seriousness, asking, "Scott, why are *you* not writing this book?" From her tone, it was 20 percent a question and 80 percent a directive.

I dismissed it out of the gate.

Thanks, but no thanks. That will never fly with the haters.

But Leigh persisted. "Scott, it's so obvious. You need to be an author on this book. In fact, you need to be the *lead* author on this book. Your passion and experience are exactly what this book needs—this is *your* book. Drop one of the potential authors; they have other talents and can't really dedicate the time to write and launch like you can. You *need* to co-author this book."

After some delicate negotiation with the CEO and executive team (most decidedly not my haters), we wrote and released *Everyone Deserves a Great Manager: The 6 Critical Practices for Leading a Team*. It debuted as a *Wall Street Journal* bestseller. I joined the two remaining leaders and authors, Todd Davis and Victoria Roos Olsson, and it put me on the map as someone who could join two other talented actors center stage.

Leigh, on that pivotal day in my Salt Lake City office, lit a spark that changed my career. And perhaps more importantly, infused a level of joy, purpose, and momentum I didn't know I desperately needed. Twenty-seven years backstage had taken a toll on me. I'd loved it, but I needed a change. Apparently, Leigh could sense it before I could. She provided the spark, and I took hold of the candle. By the way, Leigh throws cold water on most of what I say, but when she gets excited about one of my ideas, I've learned to listen up. Leigh doesn't like much, but when she does, it catches my attention.

Which is exactly what The Activator does—they boldly strike the match at the exact right moment.

Captures—Additional Tools

PRE-MENTORING REFLECTION

Consider those who have played The Activator role in your life (this might include formal mentors, colleagues, parents, friends, teachers, and ecclesiastical leaders). Review which of the Key Activator Skills illustrated in the chapter opening that they demonstrated and describe the impact in your life:

_____

_____

_____

_____

Capture the "big ideas" you have about The Activator role. Consider your own mentoring experiences. What in life has prepared you for this role? What might you need to do to prepare more? What can you adopt from the previous exercise? Write your thoughts below:

_____

_____

_____

_____

_____

IN-THE-MOMENT MENTORING PROMPTS

Revisit the questions and key insights found throughout The Activator chapter. These could include both questions for the mentee or reflection questions to help you with your mentoring mindset. Choose which feel the most relevant to an upcoming mentoring session and write them below. If the questions are reflective in nature, take a moment to answer them for yourself.

Mentee Questions

Question 1:

_____

Question 2:

_____

Role 11: The Activator

Question 3:
_____

Question 4:
_____

Mentor Reflection Questions

Question 1:
_____

Answer:
_____

Question 2:
_____

Answer:
_____

Question 3:
_____

Answer:
_____

Question 4:
_____

Answer:
_____

POST-MENTORING LEARNING

Following your mentoring session, think back to how things went when adopting The Activator role. Some roles may feel more natural to you than others, but they all benefit from objectively assessing what worked, what didn't, and what you can learn as a result.

1. *Circle the answer that best corresponds to this statement:* "The Activator role was effective for me as a mentor during the mentoring session."

   a. Strongly agree

   b. Agree

   c. Neutral

   d. Disagree

   e. Strongly disagree

2. *Circle the answer that best corresponds to this statement:* "In the mentoring session, I achieved the Activator goal: 'To ignite new levels of motivation and momentum at an intentionally impactful moment, reinforcing the mentor's faith in what their mentee can achieve.'"

   a. Strongly agree

   b. Agree

   c. Neutral

   d. Disagree

   e. Strongly disagree

3. **Explore the "why" behind your answers.** Consider what worked and didn't in your mentoring session. What should you stop or start doing? What might you do less or more of? If you found gaps in your ability to execute this role, what can you do to close them? Capture your learning from this session and anything that, on reflection, could help you grow to be more comfortable and capable in this role:

_____

_____

_____

_____

_____

Role 12:
The Connector

The Connector is an optional role where the mentor considers if, when, and how they might want to connect their mentee to their personal and professional network.

The Goal

To determine if and when a mentor will choose to provide connections to their mentee, enabling them to experience new growth, opportunities, and personal/professional development.

The Upside When The Connector Role Is Employed Well

- Creates additional opportunities for the mentee

- Leverages the mentor's network of contacts to help expedite the mentee into a new role or responsibility
- Can create a win-win for the mentee and the new mentor/ coach/employer/client
- The mentee shows great respect for and provides great value to the mentor's network, while simultaneously understanding they're in a position of privilege

The Downside When The Connector Role Is Abdicated

The mentee misses out on what could be a shortcut to the next stage of their personal/professional development and career.

Key Connector Skills

- Recognize the role is optional
- Share the importance of your network
- Make the connection (if desired)

Being a mentor is often correlated with serving in a leadership role or having significant real-world expertise. That means the chances are high you have a network of valuable personal and professional contacts that you've gained and cultivated over the years. Sometimes it's appropriate and desirable to adopt The Connector role and introduce your mentee to someone in your network. This can provide a great opportunity for a mentee to further learn, grow, and contribute in new ways. But such a tacit endorsement comes with a certain amount of risk. After all, the mentee would be leveraging *your* reputation and relationship. Their success or failure will reflect on you.

Fairly or not.

Accurately or not.

And make no mistake, you're in the middle of the mix, like it or not, once you've made the connection. So be thoughtful about whether The Connector role is a good fit for your current mentee and list of contacts.

Recognize the Role Is Optional

Playing The Connector is purely your decision. Unlike the other roles, which you will adopt repeatedly, frequently, and perhaps even more than once in the same session, The Connector is likely adopted only once in the entire mentoring relationship. Because of this, it's a solid idea to form a position on if, how, and when you might provide your mentee with connections to your own network. Be certain to articulate your position on this up front, ideally as you're employing The Boundary Setter (role #2).

Share the Importance of Your Network

It's likely you won't face this potentially awkward decision in real time with your mentee if you've done a solid job of setting the boundaries up front. In your first call or meeting, you could state, "It's important that you know, I protect access to my network with extreme care and I am going to request that you not put either of us in the uncomfortable position of you asking me for an introduction and me then needing to decline. That's a situation neither of us wants to find ourselves in."

Now that's a firm statement and could even be off-putting in an initial conversation. Like all courageous conversations in life, it depends on your delivery—your tone, pitch, timing, and intent. There are several ways I could say that same sentence and create very different moods and reactions with the recipient. Tread firmly and lightly. Whatever message you send on this topic, be sure to offer it in a way that doesn't create an antagonistic culture or the appearance of a scarce mindset up front.

Make the Connection (if Desired)

With expectations firmly established, it's completely up to you if, at any point in the mentoring relationship, you want to change or soften your position. There may well be circumstances where you know of someone in your network who's looking for an intern, a new hire, a project to invest in, or someone to coach or mentor beyond what you want or are willing and able to offer. Conversely, depending on the strength and depth of your network, you may feel comfortable making a connection that could be incrementally or even life changing to your mentee. Again, it's 100 percent your call. Here are some considerations as you hold firm or soften your position over time:

- You may treat and view your network differently than I do and have an entirely unique point of view. If so, clarify up front the level of access you're willing to offer and under what conditions.

- Perhaps you're willing to offer calibrated access correlated with the level of confidence your mentee builds in you throughout your time together. If so, state that as well.
- Communicate clearly with your connection the extent to which you've worked with and know your mentee and be candid about areas where you can't predict their success or recognize an opportunity may be a stretch. This won't get you off the hook if things go south, but might lesson the severity of the sting.

The truth is, I've been burned. My abundance and even naiveté led me to champion someone who was undeserving and came back to lessen my credibility. As I matured and my network grew and strengthened, I've become much more discerning about who I connect with whom. After all, my reputation with my network is also predicated on how insightful and transparent I am about people's competence and character. My batting average has increased as my impulsivity has decreased.

Additionally, I've been delighted with many connections I've made by putting people together, and it worked well—very well.

And if I show a shred of humility, I've been the beneficiary of people making connections for me all my life. Some I lived up to—and others not so much.

Captures—Additional Tools

PRE-MENTORING REFLECTION

Consider those who have played The Connector role in your life (this might include formal mentors, colleagues, parents, friends, teachers, and ecclesiastical leaders). Review which of the Key Connector Skills illustrated in the chapter opening that they demonstrated and describe the impact in your life:

_____

_____

_____

_____

_____

Capture the "big ideas" you have about The Connector role. Consider your own mentoring experiences. What in life has prepared you for this role? What might you need to do to prepare more? What can you adopt from the previous exercise? Write your thoughts below:

_____

_____

_____

_____

_____

IN-THE-MOMENT MENTORING PROMPTS

Revisit the questions and key insights found throughout The Connector chapter. These could include both questions for the mentee or reflection questions to help you with your mentoring mindset. Choose which feel the most relevant to an upcoming mentoring session and write them below. If the questions are reflective in nature, take a moment to answer them for yourself.

Mentee Questions

Question 1:

_____

Question 2:

_____

Question 3:

_____

Question 4:

_____

Mentor Reflection Questions

Question 1:

_____

Answer:

_____

Question 2:

_____

Answer:

_____

Question 3:

_____

Answer:

_____

Question 4:

_____

Answer:

_____

POST-MENTORING LEARNING

Following your mentoring session, think back to how things went when adopting The Connector role. Some roles may feel more natural to you than others, but they all benefit from objectively assessing what worked, what didn't, and what you can learn as a result.

1. *Circle the answer that best corresponds to this statement:* "The Connector role was effective for me as a mentor during the mentoring session."

    a. Strongly agree

    b. Agree

    c. Neutral

    d. Disagree

    e. Strongly disagree

2. *Circle the answer that best corresponds to this statement:* "In the mentoring session, I achieved the Connector goal: 'To determine if and when a mentor will choose to provide connections to their mentee, enabling them to experience new growth, opportunities, and personal/professional development.'"

    a. Strongly agree

    b. Agree

    c. Neutral

    d. Disagree

    e. Strongly disagree

3. **Explore the "why" behind your answers.** Consider what worked and didn't in your mentoring session. What should you stop or start doing? What might you do less or more of? If you found gaps in your ability to execute this role, what can you do to close them? Capture your learning from this session and anything that, on reflection, could help you grow to be more comfortable and capable in this role:

_____

_____

_____

_____

_____

Role 13:
The Closer

The Closer is the last role a mentor plays, celebrating the mentoring journey with their mentee as they formally bring the mentoring relationship to a close and point to what's next.

The Goal

Create a celebratory capstone event that closes out your mentor-mentee relationship and helps them prepare for the next part of their journey.

The Upside When The Closer Role Is Employed Well

- Follows the formal close-out process established by the sponsoring organization (if one exists)

- Establishes an important milestone representing the mentee's accomplishments
- Offers a chance to celebrate
- Creates a bridge to what's next for the mentee

The Downside When The Closer Role Is Abdicated

The mentee misses out on a chance to reflect on their progress, celebrate their wins, and turn the page on the next chapter of their journey.

Key Closer Skills

- Follow your organization's close-out process (if there is one)
- Celebrate the present
- Follow Scott's 6-Step Close-Out Process

Sadly, all good things must come to an end. And fortunately, all bad things must also come to an end.

Goodness—let's sure hope your mentoring experience isn't bad.

So, to prevent that from happening, let's talk about the importance of The Closer role.

Depending on the original structure of your mentoring plan, your close might take on different components.

Follow Your Organization's Close-Out Process (if There Is One)

My sense is that most mentors reading this book are part of an organizational mentoring initiative. Perhaps you volunteered or you might have even been "voluntold" (meaning your invitation to volunteer had some pressure behind it). Be honored if that's the case . . . I actually view being pressured into something as a massive validation of your value and talents—someone wants you! (Does not apply to junior high school vaping.) To the extent you're part of a larger mentoring initiative, there is likely a close-out process. Maybe it's a live or virtual event or some sort of celebration. Independent of that process, you as the mentor need to know when, where, and how to close—and close well.

Celebrate the Present

Let me establish I don't think we celebrate winning enough in life, like the legitimate achievement of tough goals. Take me, for example: At the time of this book's release, I will just be turning fifty-five. In the past three years, I've authored and released seven books. Many of them are bestsellers. I never celebrate. I'm too busy, too concerned maybe about grandstanding, too *something*.

Part of it is I don't live in the past or the present. I tend to only live in the future. At breakfast, I'm thinking about lunch. During tennis, I'm thinking about my flight later in the day. In a meeting, I'm thinking about church that night. When authoring a book, I'm thinking about the deadline for the release and the future contract to its sequel. I suspect it's my best hedge to ensure I control my future. But by never living in the present, I never celebrate.

I'm sure some of you reading this now think that's sad. Well, it's true (sad or not) and I bet some of you are stopped dead in your tracks and are contemplating if you also struggle with living in the present. I don't think there's a right or wrong answer. My family is both the positive recipient of me living in the future (providing for them financially, preparing for setbacks and emergencies, etc.) and the negative recipient of me not living in the present (often being somewhere else mentally—and even emotionally).

The point is, try your best to be "present in the present" during all of your mentoring meetings. Then to be focused on celebrating both the present, and the potential future, when you close out.

Follow Scott's 6-Step Close-Out Process

I have created a 6-step process for closing out your mentoring sessions:

1. *Revisit where your mentee started.* For this, the recipe book you created as The Distiller/Archivist (role #10) should be handy. During your closing celebration, hark back to where you both started by sharing notes from your opening session. Take some time to prepare for this and remind your mentee of the exact areas of growth in their mindset, behaviors, and outcomes. This is something they will never forget. Trust me. Do it and then email me their reaction at scott@scottjeffreymiller.com.

2. *Share funny/tender learnings about their growth.* No doubt your mentee has had some stalls or setbacks along the mentoring journey, or has realized you won't be naming them in your will, so some levity might be well timed. Recount some lighthearted stories that illustrate how vulnerability is a leadership, mentor, mentee, and life competency. The ability to be transparent and comfortable owning our messes, mistakes, and growth is a sign of strength. Plus, we all take ourselves way too seriously and this might be a great time to remind your mentee of that (and, more important, that our careers are not our lives).

3. *Re-identify and communicate go-forward commitments.* Now is the time to look forward. You've recapped where they started, highlighted foibles and vulnerabilities, and now you both can look to the future. What's next for your mentee? Are there key commitments they've made to themselves in the process that you might remind them of and continue to highlight their importance? Your role here is to encourage them to keep the momentum going.

4. *Resurface worthy concepts that were closed or tabled.* Now's a good time to check the parking lot you may have created where good and bad ideas go to die. Hopefully, you and they both captured items of importance and maybe a quick run-through will put these ideas to bed or surface them for another round of mentoring (with someone else).

5. *Celebrate the wins (and learn from the losses).* What will you do to celebrate? Maybe it's an invitation to check back in six months from now on a call. Perhaps it's a small gift of some sort. I even like the idea of a handmade certificate (something you drew or created yourself). I'm totally serious. Don't download a certificate from some site. Draw one. With markers and crayons and illustrate what you're certifying them in—what specifically you're awarding them with. It may seem hokey, but I promise they will keep this for the rest of their life. Take a photo of it please and email me a copy at scott@scottjeffreymiller.com. Trust me on this. The more "handmade" the better.

6. *Recap your confidence in them and outline any areas of potential support.* This is a chance for you to rehearse. Take some time before your final closing session to decide what you want to share with your mentee. Choose, with enormous care, the specific words you will use to validate them. Cite exact areas of progress or talents that have matured so they leave with these words resonating in their minds—potentially forever. Also, make it clear how/if you will offer any future support. Connections? Coaching? Becoming a reference or supporter? This is your decision, and you still get to set the boundaries for the future.

Captures—Additional Tools

PRE-MENTORING REFLECTION

Consider those who have played The Closer role in your life (this might include formal mentors, colleagues, parents, friends, teachers, and ecclesiastical leaders). Review which of the Key Closer Skills illustrated in the chapter opening that they demonstrated and describe the impact in your life:

_____

_____

_____

_____

_____

Capture the "big ideas" you have about The Closer role. Consider your own mentoring experiences. What in life has prepared you for this role? What might you need to do to prepare more? What can you adopt from the previous exercise? Write your thoughts below:

_____

_____

_____

_____

_____

IN-THE-MOMENT MENTORING PROMPTS

Revisit the questions and key insights found throughout The Closer chapter. These could include both questions for the mentee or reflection questions to help you with your mentoring mindset. Choose which feel the most relevant to an upcoming mentoring session and write them below. If the questions are reflective in nature, take a moment to answer them for yourself.

Mentee Questions

Question 1:

_____

Question 2:

_____

Question 3:

_____

Question 4:

_____

Mentor Reflection Questions

Question 1:

_____

Answer:

_____

Question 2:

_____

Answer:

_____

Question 3:

_____

Answer:

_____

Question 4:

_____

Answer:

_____

POST-MENTORING LEARNING

Following your mentoring session, think back to how things went when adopting The Closer role. Some roles may feel more natural to you than others, but they all benefit from objectively assessing what worked, what didn't, and what you can learn as a result.

1. *Circle the answer that best corresponds to this statement:* "The Closer role was effective for me as a mentor during the mentoring session."

   a. Strongly agree

   b. Agree

   c. Neutral

   d. Disagree

   e. Strongly disagree

2. *Circle the answer that best corresponds to this statement:* "In the mentoring session, I achieved the Closer goal: 'Create a celebratory capstone event that closes out your mentor-mentee relationship and helps them prepare for the next part of their journey.'"

   a. Strongly agree

   b. Agree

   c. Neutral

   d. Disagree

   e. Strongly disagree

3. **Explore the "why" behind your answers.** Consider what worked and didn't in your mentoring session. What should you stop or start doing? What might you do less or more of? If you found gaps in your ability to execute this role, what can you do to close them? Capture your learning from this session and anything that, on reflection, could help you grow to be more comfortable and capable in this role:

_____

_____

_____

_____

_____

Bonus Role 14: The Jerk

T he Jerk is exactly what not to do in a mentoring relationship. It is the abandonment of the other thirteen roles in favor of simply telling a mentee what they should do, how they should do it, and why emulating their mentor will produce the best possible life, personally and professionally. The Jerk has a ready-made answer for everything, regardless of how ineffective it might actually be.

The Goal

To take a mindless and uninformed approach to mentoring that focuses on the needs and wants of the mentor, not the mentee.

The Upside When The Jerk Role Is Employed Well

- The mentor feels validated through the mentee becoming their clone.

The Downside When The Jerk Role Is Abdicated

There is no downside to not being a Jerk.

Key Jerk Skills

- Stay focused on *your* needs as a mentor while permitting your mentee to be grateful you even make eye contact with them.
- Discourage independent thinking, as they simply need to do exactly as you say.
- Communicate that all commitments, when made by you as the mentor, are simply vague possibilities that may or may not happen, subject to competing priorities, whims, or an overabundance of disinterest.
- Never show weakness or vulnerability in front of your mentee, as you may appear human in their eyes.
- Reject boundaries of all kinds—if you'd like to introduce your mentee to your MLM side hustle—oh I'm sorry, I mean "direct sales" organization—feel free to recruit them.
- Overshare your thoughts and emotions, realizing a mentee is simply an empty bottle ready to be filled with

whatever you'd like to talk about or find interesting in the moment (no matter how inappropriate or episodic).

- Demean and berate your mentee as necessary to keep them from getting too self-confident and eventually overshadowing you and your accomplishments.
- Keep in mind that all advice is helpful advice when it comes from you, so simply having an opinion is enough grounds to share it.

And no, I won't expand on this type. Just don't be The Jerk in your mentoring relationships. (For those of you anticipating my forthcoming autobiography, congratulations! You just read it in this chapter.)

Best of success to you in your mentoring journey.

Conclusion

Feeling overwhelmed?

I know, I know . . . thirteen roles was a lot. But hey, at least The Jerk was some light reading and validated that you *aren't* one (hopefully).

Let's step back and take a look at the bigger picture. Aside from The Revealer (role #1), The Boundary Setter (role #2), and The Closer (role #13), please remember that the numbering of the roles doesn't suggest any linear order or degree of importance. Numbering is useful as chapter headers and a quick reference tool. I've turned the thirteen roles into an actual card deck for mentors to purchase and use if they'd like for this very reason. However, metaphorically, you should hold all of your mentoring cards in your hand and only deploy them as the situation warrants.

Your goal here is not mastery but awareness. You can't possibly remember all the key points about each role during a live mentoring session—nor are you expected to. I do hope, however, that you took away a few key insights from each and noted them in the Captures sections of the Chapters. With further practice and intentionality, the various nuances and differences between the roles will become more intuitive, the relevant questions more top of mind, and your ability to employ and transition between roles as part of your larger coaching and mentoring framework enhanced.

Yes, there's a lot going on here. So in review, I'll list the specific skills from each role (feel free to flip back here as a handy reference). As you read through the list, consider the skills you can most readily adopt in your mentoring sessions and those you'd like to learn or improve. Mentoring truly is a privilege, and your influence on your mentee's life can be incalculable. I wish you the very best as you work to lift another human being and help them achieve their goals (and find yourself lifted as a result).

Role 1: The Revealer

- Know the "dig site"—what the mentee is trying to accomplish and the environment in which they are trying to accomplish it in
- Employ patience and deliberate thinking
- Remain hyperaware of your own footprints (your default personality style)
- Explore with an inquisitive and gentle approach

Role 2: The Boundary Setter

- Designate duration and frequency
- Confirm the agenda

- Establish roles and responsibilities
- Set boundaries
- Call a time-out when needed
- Make and keep commitments
- Address violations
- Pull the plug if necessary

Role 3: The Absorber

- Get out of selling mode
- Avoid the "If I were you . . ." trap
- Learn your mentee's genius (and resist shaping it into yours)
- Listen and absorb as an active listener
- Practice intentional focus and empathic listening
- Stop interrupting
- Be gentle on yourself and know when to be prescriptive

Role 4: The Questioner

- Employ a laser-like focus to cut through confusion and create clarity
- Recognize that "right" is what progresses your mentee's goal
- Make it safe to share bad or embarrassing news
- Guard against "wrong" news
- Build trust and establish safety
- Avoid prosecutorial badgering
- Effectively employ "early-" and "later-" stage questions

Role 5: The Challenger

- Know *when* to challenge
- Ensure your mindset is focused on the mentee's goals and skills (not yours)
- Allow the mentee space to share
- Separate feelings from facts
- Assess your natural style on The Challenger Continuum
- Plot the right challenge level

Role 6: The Validator

- Focus on the relationship, not the issue
- Find your mentee's validation language
- Praise and validate effort
- Listen to the listening
- Recognize "validate" doesn't mean "agreeing with"

Role 7: The Navigator

- Stay a day ahead
- Connect to governing principles
- Understand the situational rules of the road
- Minimize unconscious incompetence
- Keep perspective

Role 8: The Visionary

- Speak your future truth
- Be thoughtful about what's realistically possible
- Find a new summit instead of new mountains
- Ensure it's the mentee's vision and not yours
- Calibrate your conversation

Role 9: The Flagger

- Raise the red "Stop" sign
- Raise the yellow "Caution" sign
- Choose your words carefully
- Declare your intent

Role 10: The Distiller

- Pull different "ingredients" together to create something new
- Bottle the mentoring experiences into a unique offering
- Filter out what's helpful and what's not
- Create and archive "recipes"

Role 11: The Activator

- Know which message to ignite
- Look for the signals to "strike the match"
- Use your power carefully
- Create the spark, not the candle

Role 12: The Connector

- Recognize the role is optional
- Share the importance of your network
- Make the connection (if desired)

Role 13: The Closer

- Follow your organization's close-out process (if there is one)
- Celebrate the present
- Follow Scott's 6-Step Close-Out Process

Index

Index

About
Scott Jeffrey Miller

Capping a twenty-five-year career in which he served as chief marketing officer and executive vice president, Scott Miller is currently FranklinCovey's senior advisor on thought leadership, leading the strategy, development, and publication of the firm's best-selling books.

Miller hosts the FranklinCovey-sponsored *On Leadership With Scott Miller*, the world's largest and fastest-growing weekly leadership podcast, and *C-Suite Conversations with Scott Miller*, which features interviews with the world's top executives.

Miller is the author of the multivolume series *Master Mentors: 30 Transformative Insights from Our Greatest Minds* (HarperCollins Leadership), which features insights from his interviews with the leading thinkers of our time, including Seth Godin, Susan Cain, Stedman Graham, Stephen M. R. Covey, Liz Wiseman, General Stanley McChrystal, and many others. He is the co-author of the *Wall Street Journal* bestseller *Everyone Deserves a Great Manager: The 6 Critical Practices for Leading a Team* (Simon & Schuster) and the *Mess to Success* series, including *Management Mess to Leadership Success: 30 Challenges to Become the Leader You Would Follow* and *Marketing Mess to Brand Success* (Mango Publishing).

In addition to supporting FranklinCovey's global thought leadership efforts, Miller runs Gray+Miller, a speaking, literary, and talent agency representing some of the world's foremost leaders, authors, and thinkers. He has developed the **ignite your genius™** coaching series to help leaders take their careers from accidental to deliberate, with a book of the same name launching in 2023 with Baker Publishing.

Prior to his roles as chief marketing officer and executive vice president of business development, Scott served as general manager and client partner in FranklinCovey's Chicago and UK offices. As a highly sought-after speaker and podcast guest, he has presented to hundreds of audiences across every industry and loves to share his unique journey as an unfiltered leader thriving in today's highly filtered corporate culture. Miller has also authored a leadership column for Inc.com, helmed FranklinCovey's Bookclub.com series with world-renowned authors, and hosted the weekly iHeart Radio show *Great Life, Great Career*.

Miller began his professional career in 1992 with the Disney Development Company (the real estate development division of Walt Disney Company) as a founding member of the development team that designed the town of Celebration, Florida.

Miller and his wife live in Salt Lake City, Utah, with their three sons.

More ways to *Engage* with Scott

SPEAKING & KEYNOTES

Schedule

PODCASTS & INTERVIEWS

Inquire

SCOTTJEFFREYMILLER.COM

Browse

GRAYMILLERAGENCY.COM

Visit

Learn more at: **greatmentorship.com**

Order everything your organization needs to successfully prepare your mentors!

Mentor Journal

Drawn from decades of mentoring experience, Scott designed the Mentor Journal, which includes presession and in-session worksheets to ensure your mentoring strategy is successful. The journal includes insights from the 13 roles, as well as bonus content that helps mentors easily capture conversations and track progress with their mentee. The Mentor Journal is included in the Mentorship Kit, which is available July 11 for $149.

13 Roles Reference Cards

To complement the Mentor Journal, Scott created a set of handy, quick reference cards to use in your mentoring sessions. The cards highlight key insights from each of 13 roles as well as questions, watch-outs, and phrases to progress your mentoring success. This deck of 30+ cards is paired with the Mentor Journal and comprises the Great Mentorship kit available July 11 for $149.

Learn more at: greatmentorship.com

Access Scott's Library

Management Mess to Leadership Success
RELEASED 2019
mango PUBLISHING
Amazon #1 Bestseller
The OWL AWARD

Marketing Mess to Brand Success
RELEASED 2020
mango PUBLISHING
Amazon #1 Bestseller

Everyone Deserves a Great Manager
RELEASED 2019
Simon & Schuster
Amazon #1 Bestseller
WALL STREET JOURNAL BESTSELLER

Master Mentors Volume 1
RELEASED 2021
HARPERCOLLINS LEADERSHIP
Amazon #1 Bestseller
#1 Stellar Bestseller

Master Mentors Volume 2
RELEASED 2022
HARPERCOLLINS LEADERSHIP
Amazon #1 Bestseller
#1 Stellar Bestseller

Master Mentors Volume 3
RELEASING 2024
mango PUBLISHING

The Ultimate Guide to Great Mentorship
RELEASING 2023
HARPERCOLLINS LEADERSHIP
Amazon #1 Bestseller

Career On Course
RELEASING 2024
BakerBooks

We're authors.
We're artists.
We're visionaries.

At the Gray + Miller Agency, it is our passion and expertise to amplify your voice as a visionary creator. Our clients are looking for more than a traditional talent agency; they're looking for a partner to help them brainstorm, strategize, and execute.

GMA helps visionary creators, authors, keynote speakers, artists, and entertainers bring their ideas to life through transformative experiences and published works.

GMA also thrives by connecting inspired and driven organizations to engage with today's most extraordinary talent. If you're searching for a curated collection of keynote speakers, authors, entertainers, or storytellers, you're in the right place.

We're ready to talk, so come on in, sit next to the fire, grab a cup of tea (or other cozy beverage), and let's get to know each other.

Work With Us.

graymilleragency.com

How to engage Scott in your organization's mentoring initiatives

Start with the book
Supply all your mentors with a copy of the book and invite Scott to facilitate a free, one-time, 45-60 minute book club/review as you onboard your new mentors.

Compliment your knowledge
Order for all of your mentors the quick reference printed card deck and multi-session mentoring journal to ensure their mentees are successful.

Hire Scott live in-person or virtually
Launch your mentoring initiatives by setting the vision, encouraging possibilities, and also discussing what to do when it seems to be going sideways (and how to prevent it). Invite both mentees and mentors alike!

Hire Scott to keynote
Live in-person or virtually, Scott can keynote your next event, company town hall, sales conference, or annual kick off meeting on any of his six books.

Follow or connect with Scott on social media.
LinkedIn: **Scott Jeffrey Miller** Facebook: **Scott Miller** and **Scott Jeffrey Miller (@scottmillerj1)**
Instagram: **@scottjeffreymiller** TikTok: **Scott Jeffrey Miller**
YouTube: **Scott Miller @scottmiller6504**

Tune in
Subscribe to one of Scott's two podcasts presented by FranklinCovey and watch/listen to them weekly.
franklincovey.com

Connect with other authors, artists, and visionaries
Looking to book a different speaker for your next event? Check out Scott's speaking, literary, and talent agency, Gray + Miller. **graymilleragency.com**